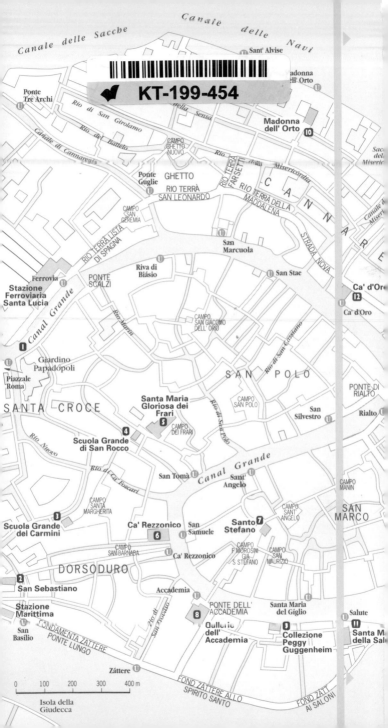

THE TOP 25 SIGHTS
THE POCKET GUIDE
CLEAR STREET MAP
WITH THE MAP

CityPack

VENICE
THE TWO-IN-ONE GUIDE

CITY MAP AND GUIDE PACK

72

CityPack
Venice

TIM JEPSON

*Tim Jepson's love of travel
began with a busking trip
through Europe, and since has
taken him from the Umbrian
countryside to the Canadian
Rockies and the windswept
tundra of the Yukon. Future
plans include walking the
length of Italy and exploring
the Arctic and South America.
Tim has written several books
for the AA, including Explorer
guides to* Canada, Rome,
Italy, Florence & Tuscany
and Venice. *Other publications
include* Rough Guides *to*
Tuscany, Canada *and* The
Pacific Northwest.

City-centre
map continues
on inside back
cover
◄

AA Publishing

Contents

About this book 4

About this book

ORGANISATION

CityPack Venice is divided into six sections to cover the six most important aspects of your visit to Venice. It includes:

- The author's view of the city and its people
- Itineraries, walks and excursions
- The top 25 sights to visit – as selected by the author
- Features about different aspects of the city that make it special
- Detailed listings of hotels, restaurants, shops and nightlife
- Practical information

In addition, easy-to-read side panels provide fascinating extra facts and snippets, highlights of places to visit and invaluable practical advice.

CROSS-REFERENCES

To help you make the most of your visit, cross-references, indicated by ►, show you where to find additional information about a place or subject.

MAPS

The fold-out map in the wallet at the back of the book is a comprehensive street plan of Venice. All the map references given in the book refer to this map. For example, the Palazzo Ducale on Piazzetta San Marco has the following information: ✚ H12 – indicating the grid square of the map in which the Palazzo Ducale will be found.

The city-centre maps found on the inside front and back covers of the book itself are for quick reference. They show the top 25 sights, described on pages 24–48, which are clearly plotted by number (**1** – **25**, not page number) from west to east.

VENICE *life*

INTRODUCING VENICE

Dangers

Contrary to popular belief, Venice is no longer sinking. Instead, it is threatened by pollution from Marghera and Mestre, two industrial towns on the mainland. Damp and salt combine with sulphur dioxide emissions to produce a corrosive brew that is lethal to stonework. Dredging and land reclamation have exacerbated the risk of flooding, a danger many do not believe will be removed by the system of steel dikes (known as MOSE) under construction across the lagoon. Having been the subject of much debate, this controversial project is now on hold awaiting further discussion. Equally damaging to Venice's long-term future is the city's dwindling population; many 'Venetians' now commute to the city from Mestre or Marghera. Schemes to preserve Venice for Venetians — modern houses, jobs, a new metro — are often at odds with those aimed at preserving the city for posterity.

Venice has been seducing visitors for centuries, its impossible watery setting and fairy-tale appearance casting a spell whose potency remains undimmed by mass tourism. More than most cities Venice repays those who make a lingering acquaintance and who show a willingness to leave the main sights in favour of the evocative quiet squares and small churches.

The city sits at the heart of a lagoon, separated from the open sea by a line of defensive sand bars. Its 118 islands, 400-plus bridges and 170 canals are divided into six districts, or *sestieri*. Half of these (San Polo, Dorsoduro and Santa Croce) lie west of the Grand Canal and half to the east (San Marco, Castello and Cannaregio). The city may seem labyrinthine, but in practice the web of streets is easier to navigate than it first appears.

Once you have grasped the city's layout, the best way to see individual attractions is in self-contained clusters. Study the map to locate the top 25 sights and ascertain which other more minor sights lie close by. Bear in mind that only three bridges cross the Grand Canal, so plan itineraries carefully to avoid unnecessary

Looking from the Piazzetta towards the Salute

walking. Also, learn to use the *traghetti* (ferries) that cross the canal at strategic points, and do not overlook the *vaporetti* (water buses) as a means of sightseeing, particularly the No. 1, which lumbers along the Grand Canal.

Choosing what to see if time is short can be hard. This said, it is best to see anything on your first morning *apart* from Piazza San Marco, the Doge's Palace or the Basilica di San Marco. Start instead with something more modest so that the crowds do not turn you against the city on your first acquaintance.

Once you have a feel for the city's intimate side you can move to the bigger draws: to the two key galleries, the Accademia and Collezione Peggy Guggenheim; to the two major churches, Santi Giovanni e Paolo and Santa Maria Gloriosa dei Frari; to the two best museums, the Correr and Ca' d'Oro; and to the finest *scuole*, the Scuola Grande di San Rocco and Scuola di San Giorgio degli Schiavoni. Thereafter, you can decide between more museums or smaller churches. Finally, you can brace yourself for the 'big two': the Palazzo Ducale (Doge's Palace) and Basilica di San Marco (St Mark's).

One-offs

Venice's best moments often occur away from the main sights. Thus you should take a boat along the Grand Canal just for the ride (➤ 24), or visit the Rialto markets at the crack of dawn before the crowds arrive (➤ 81). Alternatively, an ice cream or *cappuccino* in a square is ideal if you wish to experience the city's quieter side (➤ 54–55 and 74–75). There is little that can beat an aerial view of the city, preferably from the top of the San Giorgio Maggiore (➤ 56), and no other city offers more surprises for those who are prepared to walk and wander its streets at random (➤ 16–18).

VENICE PEOPLE

Enjoying the sun

Character

'Like the tide – six hours up and six hours down' is how one proverb summarises the Venetians' reputed tendency towards swings of character and mercurial moods. They are also supposed to be sardonic, and to feel the separateness, wistfulness and 'introspective melancholy' of an island race. Past history and isolation have also given rise to an un-Italian instinct for co-operation and sense of civic pride. Venetians are also polite and reserved, even in the face of their city's invasion by tourists. Other Italians think them wily, cunning and clever in speech. They are also considered lazy (wrongly), and are said to enjoy their wine more than they should...

Many Venetians start their day on a boat or train. Some commute from the mainland, leaving their cars in the vast car parks at the end of Venice's only 'road' – the causeway that crosses the lagoon from Mestre (officially a part of 'Venice'). Others board the water buses (*vaporetti*) that ply the city's canals, heading to work, school or university in a city where even the traffic jams are beautiful. Breakfast for most is a hurried *espresso* and *brioche* (croissant) at one of the city's many small bars.

Mid-morning sees Venetian mothers at large, either shopping in the Rialto markets or chatting to friends as their children play in the city's palace-lined squares. This is also the time when a veritable army of old women hits the streets to walk their dogs. Lunchtime leads to another rush-hour on the water as people return home for lunch, battling with tourists for a place on the laden *vaporetti*. Some head for Venice's traditional *enoteche*, where a glass of wine and light meal take the place of the traditional long lunch.

In the dog-days of summer, the afternoons pass slowly as Venetians wisely keep to their houses to escape the heat of the sun. Those not so lucky might instead take an *ombra*, or 'shadow', the name given to the Venetian habit of breaking off work for a glass of wine in one of the cave-like *bacari* (wine bars) that cluster in certain parts of the city. Later on, people might sip an aperitif or Prosecco, a local sparkling wine, before heading home.

Evenings are sedate. Most Venetians prefer a meal at home with friends or a quiet drink to a meal out or a boisterous night of dancing. Venice has little nightlife, so for entertainment many locals head across the water to Mestre. Others content themselves with dinner, preferably in a restaurant undiscovered by tourists, or a stroll followed by an ice cream or *digestif* in one of the city's café-ringed squares.

VENICE IN FIGURES

Geography
- Latitude: 41°N
- Longitude: 12°E
- Height above sea-level: 80cm
- Height of 1966 floods: 2m
- Highest point: Campanile (90.5m)
- Average January temperature: 3.8°C
- Average July temperature: 23.6°C
- Average January rainfall: 58mm
- Average July rainfall: 37mm

People
- Population after 1630 plague: 102,000
- Population in 1938: 164,000
- Population in 1994: 72,000
- Population under 10 in 1994: 4,530
- Population over 60 in 1994: 23,300
- Average age in 1994: 44
- Population of Mestre in 1938: 65,000
- Population of Mestre in 1990: 192,000
- People leaving Venice annually: 1,500
- Cost of living: 1 per cent higher than Milan and 3 per cent higher than Rome
- Local workforce involved in tourism: over 50 per cent
- Number of souvenir shops: around 450
- Number of plumbers: under 20

City
- Official age in 2000: 1,579 years
- Distance from west to east: 5km
- Distance from north to south: 2km
- Size equivalent to: New York's Central Park
- Number of alleys (estimate): 3,000
- Length of alleys if laid end to end: 200km
- Number of street cats in 1994: 2,327
- Number of bridges (estimate): 400
- Number of islands: 118
- Number of canals: 170
- Annual rate of sinking: 0cm
- Year sinking stopped: 1983
- Visitors per year (estimate): 12,000,000
- Most visitors in one day (estimate): 150,000 (on 15 July 1989)
- Number of homes without bathrooms: 2,000
- Amount of sulphur dioxide gas produced by Marghera's factories: 50,000 tonnes per year
- Buildings on Grand Canal with damaged foundations: 60 per cent

9

A CHRONOLOGY

800 BC | Sporadic settlement of the lagoon by the Venetii and Euganei tribes.

250 BC | Rome conquers north-eastern Italy (*Venetia*) and founds important colonies at Padua, Verona, Altinium and Aquileia.

AD 402 | Alaric the Goth sacks Altinium and other north-eastern colonies. A vision of the Virgin guides refugees to an island in the lagoon.

421 | According to legend Venice is founded on 25 March, the Feast Day of the Virgin Mary.

453 | Aquileia is sacked by Attila the Hun, prompting another exodus of refugees to the lagoon.

466 | The lagoon's settlements elect 'maritime tribunes' to co-ordinate policy.

697 | Paoluccio Anafesto, traditional first doge ('leader'), is elected.

726 | The first documented doge, Orso Ipato, rules the lagoon from the now-vanished colony of Heraclea.

810 | Lagoon dwellers gather on the more easily defended islands of the Rivus Altus (Rialto).

814 | Work begins on the Doge's Palace.

828 | Venetian merchants steal the relics of St Mark from Alexandria.

829 | Work begins on the Basilica di San Marco

1099 | Venice provides ships for the First Crusade.

1171 | Venice's six districts, or *sestieri*, are founded.

1173 | Work begins on the first Rialto bridge.

1204 | Venice sacks Constantinople and acquires much of the former Byzantine Empire.

1269 | Marco Polo leaves Venice to travel in the East.

1309	Work begins on the present Doge's Palace.
1348	The Black Death kills half the population.
1380	Victory over the Genoese wins Venice naval supremacy in the Adriatic and Mediterranean.
1406	Venice defeats Padua and Verona to lay the foundations of a mainland empire.
1430	Birth of Giovanni Bellini, one of Venice's greatest Renaissance painters.
1453	Venice's power is at its height, but the Turks take Constantinople.
1498	Vasco da Gama's discovery of the Cape route to the East weakens Venice's trading monopolies.
1571	Venice loses Cyprus to the Turks.
1669	The Turks take Crete from the Venetians.
1678	The composer Antonio Vivaldi is born in Venice.
1718	The loss of Morea marks the end of Venice's maritime empire.
1797	Napoleon invades Italy: the last doge abdicates and the Venetian Republic comes to an end.
1814	After Napoleon's defeat, the Congress of Vienna cedes Venice and the Veneto to Austria.
1848	Daniele Manin leads an unsuccessful Venetian uprising against Austrian rule.
1866	Venice joins a united Italy.
1902	The Campanile in Piazza San Marco collapses
1966	Devastating floods ravage Venice.
1988	Works begins on the lagoon's flood barrier known as MOSE.

11

PEOPLE & EVENTS FROM HISTORY

Antonio Vivaldi

Vivaldi was born in Venice in 1678, the son of a violinist. Although ordained as a priest, he devoted much of his life to music, teaching the violin at La Pietà, an

orphanage whose girls received music training as part of their state-funded education (in time such orphanages became renowned as centres of musical excellence). La Pietà's resident orchestra enabled him to create a wealth of musical compositions, including 50 operas and 454 concertos, as well as the famous 'Four Seasons'. Although praised at the height of his career, his star soon waned, and in 1740 he was forced to leave Venice for Vienna to seek work.

He died a year later and received only a pauper's funeral.

CASANOVA

Casanova was born in Venice in 1725. Although destined for the priesthood, his adolescent follies saw him expelled from his seminary. He was then exiled from Venice for five years, during which time he travelled between Paris, Dresden, Prague and Vienna. On his return in 1755 he was imprisoned on charges of sorcery. In 1756, after 15 months in the Palazzo Ducale's prisons, he made a daring escape to France, where he introduced Paris to the lottery before being forced to flee from angry creditors. He then visited London, Berlin, St Petersburg and Warsaw, but was forced to leave the last after a duel. After a period in Spain he returned to Venice, where he became a spy for the Inquisition. A libel suit forced his departure from the city, and he spent his remaining years as a librarian for a Bohemian count.

MARCO POLO

Marco Polo was born in Venice around 1254, the son of a merchant adventurer. In 1269 he joined his father on a journey that would last over 20 years. He travelled through present-day Turkey and Palestine, crossed the deserts of eastern Iran and Afghanistan, and in 1275 arrived at the court of Kublai Khan. Over the next 17 years he served the Mongol emperor, travelling widely in China and the Far East on a series of diplomatic and trade missions. In 1292 he decided to head for home, travelling to Venice by way of Vietnam, Malaysia, Sumatra and Sri Lanka. In 1298, three years after his return, he was captured by the Genoese at the Battle of Curzola. While in a Genoa prison he met a Pisan scribe, Rusticello, to whom he dictated the popular *Description of the World* (now better known as *Il Milione*), an account of his 25 years in the Far East.

VENICE
how to organise your time

ITINERARIES

Distances in Venice are not great, but it still makes sense to see sights in self-contained clusters. Try to avoid visiting St Mark's and the Doge's Palace – both likely to be extremely busy – on your first morning.

Pay attention to opening times, especially those of churches (➤ 87), which very rarely correspond in actuality to those advertised. Generally churches are open mid- or late afternoons.

ITINERARY ONE	**SAN POLO**
Morning	Scuola Grande dei Carmini (➤ 26)
	Chiesa dei Carmini (➤ 26)
	San Sebastiano (➤ 25)
	San Nicolò dei Mendicoli (➤ 53)
	San Pantalon (➤ 53)
	Santa Maria Gloriosa dei Frari (➤ 28)
Afternoon	Scuola Grande di San Rocco (➤ 27)
	San Polo (➤ 53)
	Campo San Polo (➤ 55)
	San Giacomo dell'Orio (➤ 52)
ITINERARY TWO	**SAN MARCO**
Morning	Ponte di Rialto and Rialto markets (➤ 81)
	Boat ride on Canal Grande to San Marco (➤ 24)
	Piazza San Marco (➤ 36)
	Campanile (➤ 38)
	Basilica di San Marco (➤ 39)
	Museo Civico Correr (➤ 37)
Afternoon	Palazzo Ducale (➤ 40)
	San Zaccaria (➤ 45)
	San Giovanni in Bragora (➤ 47)
	Boat (No. 82) to San Giorgio Maggiore (➤ 44)
	Boat (No. 82) from San Giorgio to the Giudecca, then to Piazzale Roma
ITINERARY THREE	**CASTELLO**
Morning	Santa Maria Formosa (➤ 42)
	San Zaccaria (➤ 45)
	San Francesco della Vigna (➤ 52)
	Scuola di San Giorgio degli Schiavoni (➤ 46)
	San Giovanni in Bragora (➤ 47)

The Campanile and Palazzo Ducale

15

WALKS

The Rialto bridge

INFORMATION

Distance 3km (1.5km to San Nicolò, 1.5km to Salute)
Time 2–5 hours
Start point Ponte di Rialto
➕ G11
🚋 Rialto 1, 3, 82
End point Piazza San Marco
➕ G12
🚋 San Marco 1, 3, 4, 82
🕐 Opening hours vary
🍴 Campo Santa Margherita, Campo San Polo and Campo Santo Stefano (Campo Francesco Morosini) (➤ 54–55)

FROM THE RIALTO TO PIAZZA SAN MARCO

Walk north from the Rialto bridge up Ruga degli Orefici. Turn left on Ruga Vecchia San Giovanni and follow it west to Campo San Polo. From the square's south-western corner follow the alleys to Campo San Tomà. From here, head to Campo dei Frari and follow Calle Scaleter and Calle San Pantalon to Campo San Pantalon and Campo Santa Margherita. From the latter, either walk to Campo San Barnaba along Rio Terrà Canal, or loop west from Campo dei Carmini to take in San Sebastiano and perhaps San Nicolò dei Mendicoli. Return to Campo San Barnaba on Calle d'Avogaria and Calle Lunga San Barnaba, then follow Calle dei Casini and Calle della Toletta to the Accademia. Here you might divert south to the Záttere ai Gesuati and then east to Punta della Dogana, returning to the

Accademia via Santa Maria della Salute. Otherwise, cross the Ponte dell'Accademia to Campo Santo Stefano (Campo Francesco Morosini).

Walk east on Calle Spezier into Campo San Maurizio. Continue east to Campo San Moisè via Campo Santa Maria Zobenigo and Calle Larga (Viale) XXII Marzo. Beyond San Moisè, turn right down Calle Vallaresso and follow the waterfront east to Piazza San Marco.

FROM PIAZZA SAN MARCO THROUGH THE CITY'S QUIETER NORTHERN DISTRICTS TO THE FERROVIA

Walk east from Piazza San Marco to Campo di San Zaccaria via either the Riva degli Schiavoni and Calle San Zaccaria, or Calle della Canonica and Campo Santi Filippo e Giacomo. From the north-western corner of Campo San Zaccaria, take Calle San Provolo north and then turn left

Piazza San Marco

on to Corte Rotta (this turns into Ruga Giuffa) to reach Campo Santa Maria Formosa. Take Calle Lunga Santa Maria Formosa off the eastern side of the square and follow it to Calle Ospedale and Salizzada Santi Giovanni e Paolo. Turn left here to reach the church and Campo di Santi Giovanni e Paolo. Proceed west on Calle Larga G Gallina to Campo Santa Maria Nova, detouring south briefly to see Santa Maria dei Miracoli.

Continue north-west through Campo San Canciano. Shortly before reaching Campo Santi Apostoli, turn right on Calle Muazzo and Rio Terrà dei Santi Apostoli towards Campo dei Gesuiti. Turn left to follow Fondamenta Zen west along the canal. Turn left at the end (Calle della Racchetta) and then take the third right (Sottopasseggio dei Preti).

Turn right on Fondamenta di San Felice and then left on to Fondamenta della Misericordia. At Calle Larga turn right to Campo dei Mori and Madonna dell'Orto. Return south to Fondamenta degli Ormesini and cross the Rio della Misericordia canal to reach Campo di Ghetto Nuovo, the heart of Venice's fascinating old Jewish ghetto. Explore the area and then head south-west to Fondamenta Pescaria. Cross the Canale di Cannaregio into Campo San Geremia and follow Rio Terrà di Lista di Spagna to the railway station (Ferrovia).

THE SIGHTS

- Piazza San Marco (➤ 36)
- Palazzo Ducale (➤ 40)
- San Zaccaria (➤ 45)
- Santa Maria Formosa (➤ 42)
- Santi Giovanni e Paolo (➤ 43)
- Campo Santi Giovanni e Paolo (➤ 54)
- Santa Maria dei Miracoli (➤ 41)
- I Gesuiti (➤ 52)
- Campo dei Mori (➤ 54)
- Madonna dell'Orto (➤ 33)

INFORMATION

Distance 3.25km
Time 2–4 hours
Start point Piazza San Marco
✚ G12
🚏 San Marco 1, 3, 4, 82
End point Railway station (Ferrovia)
🚉 D10
🚏 Ferrovia 1, 3, 4, 82
🕐 Opening hours vary
🍴 Campo Santa Maria Formosa (➤ 55)

EVENING STROLLS

INFORMATION

San Marco
Distance 0.5km
Time 10–15 minutes
Start point Riva degli Schiavoni or
Piazza San Marco
✚ G12
▱ San Marco or San Zaccaria 1,
3, 4, 52, 82
End point Campo Santo Stefano
(Campo Francesco Morosini)
or Ponte dell'Accademia
✚ F12
▱ Accademia 1, 3, 4, 82

San Polo
Distance 1.25km
Time 20–25 minutes
Start point Ponte di Rialto
✚ G11
▱ Rialto 1, 3, 82
End point Campo Santa Margherita
✚ D12
▱ Ca' Rezzonico 1

Santa Maria della Salute
at sunset

SAN MARCO

Recommending an evening stroll in Venice is not easy, for almost any combination of alleys and streets offers a magical and memorable experience. Water laps quietly in the canals, streets are mostly empty and deathly quiet (but perfectly safe), and every shadow hides a special secret. If you want some life, however, and the promise of an aperitif at the end of your stroll, try walking from Piazza San Marco to Campo Santo Stefano (Campo Francesco Morosini). Exit the Piazza at the west end (or walk round by the water and the Giardinetti Reali) and follow Calle Larga (Viale) XXII Marzo and Calle delle Ostreghe to Campo Santa Maria Zobenigo. Then walk through Campo San Maurizio into Campo Santo Stefano (Campo Francesco Morosini), where you can either take time out at Paolin (➤ 75) or walk to the Ponte dell'Accademia for views of the Grand Canal and the Salute.

SAN POLO

Start at the Ponte di Rialto by admiring the streetlife of the Rialto: day-trippers returning home, people crowding into waterside restaurants, and the constant coming and going of gondolas. Then walk west along the Fondamenta del Vin and turn right through Campo San Silvestro to Campo Sant'Aponal. From here, turn left along Calle di Mezzo to Campo San Polo, one of Venice's largest squares,

where the chances are there will be people doing much the same as you are (several bars here have outside tables so that patrons can watch the world go by). Next, take Salizzada San Polo and follow the streets west to Campo San Tomà. Turn north towards the Frari and then west towards San Pantalon. From here, walk over the bridge into Campo Santa Margherita, another lively square with several pleasant bars and cafés (➤ 54–55).

ORGANISED SIGHTSEEING

AMERICAN EXPRESS TOURS

Although several firms offer organised sight-seeing tours, the best-known trips are arranged by American Express. The company offers two city tours daily, one in the morning and the other in the afternoon. The tours last two hours and cost around L40,000 for the morning tour and L45,000 for the afternoon, with a reduction if you book for both. Trips start from outside the American Express office, though you should call ahead to confirm current prices and timings.

🔲 G12 ✉ Salizzada San Moisè, San Marco 1471 ☎ 041 520 0844

The morning tour is known as the 'Jewels of the Venetian Republic Tour' and visits, among other sights, the Basilica di San Marco, the Campanile and the Palazzo Ducale. The second tour visits several palaces and churches, including the Frari, and ends at the Rialto bridge after a gondola ride to the Ca' d'Oro. American Express also offers an evening tour, the 'Evening Serenade' (twice nightly in summer and once in winter), which costs L50,000 and involves a 50-minute ride in a gondola with musicians and singers, and departs from Piazza Santa Maria del Giglio. It also runs, along with several other companies, much more expensive trips to mainland towns such as Padua, as well as boat and coach trips to see the Palladian villas dotted along the Brenta Canal. Book these a day in advance.

Another tour heads out to the Venetian lagoon and islands, a three-hour trip with two departures daily (morning and afternoon) that takes in Murano, Torcello and Burano. Tours depart from the Riva degli Schiavoni. On the whole it is best to avoid some of the other commercialised tours, especially to Murano, as much emphasis is placed on visiting glass factories with a view to selling you their products. You might consider Cooperativa San Marco tours, which can be booked through travel agents or direct from the booth on the quayside by the Giardinetti Reali.

Guides

Venice has numerous multi-lingual guides who can be hired by the half-day, full day or week, as well as gondoliers and drivers for hire. American Express (see main text) organises both guides and gondoliers, or you can choose one yourself by contacting the Guides' Association (🔲 G11 ✉ Calle Morosini della Regina, 750 San Marco ☎ 041 520 9038). The main tourist office in the Palazzetto Selva (➤ 87) also has details of guides, as well as information on organised tours. Bookings for trips usually have to be made directly or through travel agents, of which there are many around the city.

Bound for one of the islands of the lagoon

19

EXCURSIONS

Murano glass

MURANO

Murano is known primarily for its glass, Venice's glass furnaces having been moved to the island in 1291 as a precaution against fire. Though not as pretty as the lagoon's other major islands (see below for Burano and Torcello), it has three major sights over and above its ubiquitous glass workshops and showrooms (most of the latter are on the island's main street, Fondamenta dei Vetrai). The first is the church of San Pietro Martire, noted for the superb wooden carvings (1652–6) in its sacristy and Giovanni Bellini's glorious altarpiece (second altar on the right) of the *Madonna and Child with Doge Barbarigo and Sts Mark and Augustine* (1488). Also well worth seeing is the Museo Vetrario, Italy's only glass museum, with displays dating from Roman times to the present day. Just beyond lies the church of Santa Maria e Donato, its exterior distinguished by a striking arched and colonnaded apse. Inside, the 12th-century apse mosaic of the Madonna is outstanding, as are the swirling coloured patterns of the lovely mosaic floor (1141).

BURANO

If Murano is known for its glass, Burano is equally lauded for its lace. Breathtakingly intricate examples of traditional lace can be seen in the Scuola (or Museo) di Merletti, which also allows you to watch local women working according to traditional methods. Unlike Murano, Burano is attractive to visit for its own sake. The island's fame in part rests on its many brightly painted houses, whose wonderful primary colours make its streets and canals as picturesque as any in Venice itself.

Fishing boats are still moored at the island's fringes, while nets are laid out to dry on the pavements, features which – despite the faint air of commercialism and the many visitors – still lend the island the feel of a genuine fishing community. At little more than half a kilometre across, the island is also easy to explore, and as a day-trip it makes the perfect accompaniment to Torcello, which lies just five minutes away by boat (see below).

Torcello

TORCELLO

The island of Torcello is one of the most magical places in Venice. Although now all but deserted, it was probably the city's birthplace and the first area of the lagoon settled in the 5th century. Malaria and the silting up of its canals put paid to its prosperity in the 12th century, double blows from which it never recovered. Today it is home to little more than a single hamlet and a beautiful patchwork of green fields and tree-shaded canals. Dominating its huddle of houses is the cathedral of Santa Maria Assunta, Venice's oldest building (founded 639). The cathedral is one of Venice's loveliest sights and is the finest Veneto-Byzantine church in Italy. The simple interior is filled with outstanding works of art, chief of which are the 12th-century apse mosaic of the Madonna (the 11th-century frieze below shows the Apostles) and the graphic 12th-century mosaic of the Last Judgement on the rear wall. Almost equally remarkable are the 7th-century high altar, the 11th-century mosaics to its right, and the beautiful rood screen and choir, the former supporting a painted balcony of the *Virgin and Apostles*. Also worth seeing close by are the Byzantine church of Santa Fosca – beautiful if rather over-restored – and the small Museo dell'Estuario, a museum whose exhibits are devoted to many aspects of the area's long history.

INFORMATION

Torcello

✚ Off map

☎ Santa Maria Assunta and Santa Fosca 041 730084. Museo dell'Estuario 041 730761

🕐 Santa Maria Assunta and Santa Fosca daily 10–12:30, 2–5. Museo dell'Estuario Tue–Sun 10:30–12:30, 2–4:30 (winter 10–12:30, 2–4)

🚤 12 from the Fondamente Nuove (every 60–90 minutes). The journey takes 45 minutes. Catch the first boat of the day to avoid the crowds

✋ Santa Maria Assunta cheap. Santa Fosca free. Museo dell'Estuario cheap

Practicalities

The *Biglietto Isole*, a single one-way ticket, enables you to visit Murano, Burano and Torcello with stop-overs *en route*, though a cheaper additional ticket is required for the return to Venice from either Burano or Torcello. Boats usually call at Burano first, except early in the morning and during weekends in the high season, when they dock at Torcello. If returning to Venice from Torcello, check that the boat is returning directly to the city rather than taking a longer route home via Treporti, Punta Sabbioni and the Lido. Burano has several good restaurants and many bars and cafés, while Torcello has one expensive restaurant, a middling trattoria and two small bars (➤ 68–76), but there are plenty of picnic spots.

What's On

February	*Carnevale* (Carnival): Pageants, masks and fancy dress (ten days leading up to Shrove Tuesday).
March	*Su e zo per i ponti*: A long street race for serious and fun runners alike in which competitors run 'up and down the bridges' of Venice (second Sunday of the month).
April	*Festa di San Marco*: The feast day of Venice's patron saint is marked by a gondola race from Sant'Elena to the Punta della Dogana. Men traditionally give women a red rose.
May	*La Sensa*: Venice's mayor re-enacts the Marriage to the Sea, in which the doge would cast a ring into the sea to symbolise the 'wedding' of the city to the sea (Sunday after Ascension Day).
	Vogalonga: Literally the 'long row', a 32km race from Piazza San Marco to Burano and back; many hundreds of different boats take part (Sunday following La Sensa).
June	*Biennale*: Venice's international art exhibition takes place every odd-numbered year (June–September).
July	*Festa del Redentore*: Pontoons are laid across the Giudecca canal to the Redentore to celebrate Venice's deliverance from the plague of 1576. People picnic in boats and there is a fireworks display (third Sunday of the month).
September	*Venice Film Festival*: International festival held on the Lido (early September).
	Regata Storica: Historical costume pageant and procession of boats on the Canal Grande, followed by a race between gondoliers and other oarsmen (first Sunday of the month).
November	*Festa della Salute*: A pontoon is built across the Canal Grande to the Salute to celebrate the passing of a plague in 1630 (21 November).

VENICE's
top 25 sights

The sights are showm on the maps on the inside front cover and inside back cover, and are numbered **1–25** from west to east across the city.

CANAL GRANDE

HIGHLIGHTS

- Palazzo Vendramin-Calergi
- San Stae
- Ca' Pesaro
- Ca' d'Oro
- Ponte di Rialto

INFORMATION

- C10–G13
- 1, 82 (year round); 3, 4 (summer only)
- Good
- Moderate
- Scuola Grande di San Rocco (➤ 27), Santa Maria Gloriosa dei Frari (➤ 28), Ca' Rezzonico (➤ 29), Gallerie dell'Accademia (➤ 31), Ca d'Oro (➤ 35), Piazza San Marco (➤ 36)
- *Vaporetto* 1 halts at every stop; 82 stops at Piazzale Roma, Ferrovia, San Marcuola, Rialto, San Tomà, San Samuele and Accademia; 3 stops at Rialto, San Samuele and Accademia; and 4 stops at Accademia and San Samuele

Regata Storica

There's no better introduction to the magic of Venice than a boat trip down the Grand Canal. The world's most beautiful 'street', an endlessly unfolding pageant with superb views of the city's finest palaces and a fascinating insight into Venetian life.

Bustle Snaking through the heart of Venice, the Grand Canal divides the city into two: three of the city's six districts, or *sestieri*, lie to one side and three to the other. At most hours of the day and night it is alive with boats and bustle of all description, providing an almost hypnotic spectacle when admired from one of its three bridges (the Scalzi, Rialto and Accademia) or from the heavily laden *vaporetti* that ply up and down its 4km length. In addition to the life of the canal is the attraction of the palaces that line its banks, a 500-year-old digest of some of the city's most appealing architecture.

Boats A trip along this intriguing canal is a pleasure in itself, and one that you can never tire of. The best thing to do is to board either *vaporetto* No. 1 or No. 82 at Piazzale Roma or the Ferrovia (railway station), making sure the boat is heading in the right direction. For the best view, try to secure one of the few outside seats at the front or rear of the boat: Venetians prefer to stand in the middle. The Rialto and Accademia bridges make convenient breaks in the journey, but for your first trip it is a good idea to stay aboard all the way to San Marco (and then perhaps make a return trip to take in the splendour of the palaces on the opposite bank). It is also well worth making the journey at night, when this experience, if anything, is even more magical.

SAN SEBASTIANO

While paintings by some of Venice's artists – notably Titian and Tintoretto – are often showcased in grandiose settings, the city's finest collection of works by Veronese is gathered in the humble little church of San Sebastiano.

Veronese Born in Verona, Paolo Caliari Veronese (1528–88) moved to Venice while he was in his twenties, settling close to San Sebastiano, which soon became his parish church. In 1555 he was commissioned to decorate the church's sacristy, where he left paintings of the *Evangelists* and the *Coronation of the Virgin*. Impressed by his work, the church authorities gave him free rein to decorate the church's ceiling, and he produced a sumptuous collection of paintings, gilt and elaborate stucco (much of the decoration was carried out by Veronese's brother, Benedetto). The three main panels depict episodes from the Old Testament story of Esther, chosen for its symbolic parallels with the stories of Eve and the Virgin Mary.

Monopoly The hand of Veronese can also be seen in the choir, where he painted the high altarpiece – the *Madonna and Child with Sts Sebastian, Peter, Francis and Catherine* (1570) – and the two vast paintings on the north and south walls. The latter portray *Sts Mark and Marcellinus Led to Martyrdom and Comforted by St Sebastian* and *The Second Martyrdom of St Sebastian* (Sebastian survived his first assault by arrows and was martyred by being pummelled to death). Veronese also painted *The Trial and Martyrdom of St Sebastian* in the nuns' choir, an unusual gallery above the church's west end. He even designed the organ and painted its door panels, his decorative monopoly of San Sebastiano making it only fitting that he was buried here: his tomb, and that of his brother, lie in front of the chapel to the left of the choir.

HIGHLIGHTS

- Sacristy
- Ceiling
- Nuns' choir
- Choir
- Organ
- *St Nicholas* (1563), Titian (first chapel on right)
- *Madonna and Child* (16th century), Tommaso Lombardo (second chapel on right)
- *Tomb of Archbishop Podocattaro of Cyprus* (d1555), Sansovino (fourth chapel on right)

INFORMATION

- C13
- Campo San Sebastiano
- 041 282487 or 041 275 0462
- Daily 10–2, 4–6
- Campo Santa Margherita and Campo San Barnaba
- San Basilio 82
- Good
- Cheap
- Scuola Grande dei Carmini (➤ 26), Scuola Grande di San Rocco (➤ 27), Santa Maria Gloriosa dei Frari (➤ 28), Ca' Rezzonico (➤ 29), Gallerie dell'Accademia (➤ 31)
- Restoration work or staff shortages may alter opening times

3

SCUOLA GRANDE DEI CARMINI

INFORMATION

- D12
- Campo dei Carmini, Campo Santa Margherita
- 041 528 9420
- Mon–Sat 9–12, 3–6
- Campo Santa Margherita
- Ca' Rezzonico 1
- Poor: stairs to main rooms
- Moderate
- San Sebastiano (➤ 25), Scuola Grande di San Rocco (➤ 27), Santa Maria Gloriosa dei Frari (➤ 28), Ca' Rezzonico (➤ 29), Gallerie dell'Accademia (➤ 31), Campo Santa Margherita (➤ 54)
- Visit the adjacent Chiesa dei Carmini (☎ 041 522 6553 🕑 Mon–Sat 7:30–noon, 3–7; Sun 4:30–7:30)

Giovanni Battista Tiepolo's paintings are not to all tastes, but those in the intimate little Scuola Grande dei Carmini – all pastel shades and fleshy figures – are a pleasant change from the more obvious drama of Titian or Tintoretto.

Carmelites The Carmelite Order's Venetian chapter was originally installed in Santa Maria del Carmelo (or Carmini), the Carmelite church just to the left of the *scuola* (see below). In 1667 the order commissioned Baldassare Longhena, one of the era's leading architects, to design a new home in the present building (Longhena also designed Santa Maria della Salute and a number of palaces on the Grand Canal). The façade, though hampered by its cramped site, is known for its rigorous symmetry and many masks and projections, all features favoured by architects of the period.

Paintings The highlights are Giovanni Battista Tiepolo's nine ceiling paintings (1739–44) in the Salone, a large room on the first floor reached via an extravagantly stuccoed staircase. The paintings' central panel depicts the vision of St Simon Stock elected the Carmelites' prior-general in 1247, in which the Virgin appears to the saint with a 'scapular'. This garment of two linked pieces of cloth became central to Carmelite belief as wearers were promised relief from the pains of purgatory on the 'first Sunday after death'. Two adjacent rooms, the Albergo and Archivio, feature heavy wooden ceilings and several paintings, the best of which is Piazzetta's *Judith and Holofernes* (1743). Be sure to visit the Chiesa dei Carmini to see Lorenzo Lotto's *St Nicholas of Bari* (1529), located by the side door (second chapel), and Cima da Conegliano's fine *Nativity* (1509) above the second altar on the opposite (south) wall.

SCUOLA GRANDE DI SAN ROCCO

In a city of superlative and often striking works of art, there can be few that have made such a marked and powerful first impression than the colossal cycle of 54 paintings by Tintoretto that line the walls of the Scuola Grande di San Rocco.

Scuola This *scuola*, formerly a charitable institution for the sick, was founded in 1478 in honour of St Roch, a saint whose efficacy against disease made him popular in pestilence-ridden Venice. In 1564, having become one of the city's wealthiest confraternities, the *scuola* instigated a competition to decorate the walls of its meeting place. It was won by Tintoretto, who then spent some 23 years creating one of Europe's greatest painting cycles.

Albergo To see Tintoretto's 54 paintings in the order they were painted, ignore the canvases on the ground floor and in the main hall (Sala Grande) up the stairs. Instead, make for the Sala dell'Albergo (off the main hall), dominated by a huge *Crucifixion* (1565), often described as one of Italy's greatest paintings. The room's central ceiling panel is *St Roch in Glory*, the painting that won Tintoretto his commission. Moving into the main hall the ceiling paintings (1575–81) describe episodes from the Old Testament, all carefully chosen to draw parallels with the *scuola*'s charitable or curative aims. The ten wall paintings show scenes from the New Testament. Note the superb 17th-century wooden carvings around the walls, by the little-known sculptor Francesco Pianta. Of the eight paintings downstairs, the artist's last in the *scuola* (1583–8), the best are the idiosyncratic *Annunciation* and *The Flight into Egypt*.

HIGHLIGHTS

- Crucifixion
- Moses Strikes Water from the Rock
- The Fall of Manna
- The Temptation of Christ
- The Adoration of the Shepherds
- Wooden sculptures
- The Flight into Egypt
- Annunciation

Tintoretto's Crucifixion

INFORMATION

- ✚ E11
- ✉ Campo San Rocco
- ☎ 041 523 4864
- 🕐 May–Oct: daily 9–5:30. Nov–Apr: Mon–Fri 10–1; Sat–Sun 10–4
- 🍴 Campo dei Frari
- 🚣 San Tomà 1, 82
- ♿ Poor
- 💷 Moderate
- ↔ San Sebastiano (➤ 25), Scuola Grande dei Carmini (➤ 26), Santa Maria Gloriosa dei Frari (➤ 28), Accademia (➤ 31)
- ❓ A free leaflet to the *scuola*'s paintings is usually available with your ticket

27

5

SANTA MARIA GLORIOSA DEI FRARI

HIGHLIGHTS

- *Madonna and Child*, Giovanni Bellini
- *Assumption*, Titian
- *Madonna di Ca' Pesaro*, Titian
- *Madonna and Child* (1339), Paolo Veneziano (sacristy)
- *St John the Baptist*, Donatello
- *Mausoleo Tiziano* (Tomb of Titian)
- *Monumento a Iacopo Marcello* (d 1484)
- Wooden choir (124 stalls)
- *Monumento al Doge Giovanni Pesaro*
- *Monumento al Canova*

INFORMATION

- ✚ E11
- ✉ Campo dei Frari
- ☎ 041 522 2637
- 🕐 Mon–Sat 9–6; Sun 10:30–6
- 🍴 Campo dei Frari
- 🚊 San Tomà 1, 82
- ♿ Good: one or two steps
- 💰 Cheap; free on Sun
- ↔ San Sebastiano (➤ 25), Scuola Grande dei Carmini (➤ 26), Scuola Grande di San Rocco (➤ 27), Ca' Rezzonico (➤ 29), Gallerie dell'Accademia (➤ 31)

If you were allowed to walk away with just one work of art from Venice it could well be Giovanni Bellini's sublime altarpiece in Santa Maria Gloriosa dei Frari – although two other paintings in this magnificent Gothic church are contenders.

Church The 'Frari' narrowly outrivals Santi Giovanni e Paolo as Venice's largest and most important church. Founded around 1250, it became the mother church of the city's Franciscans, after whom it is named – *frari* is a Venetian corruption of *frati*, meaning 'friars'.

Tombs Many of the city's great and good are buried in the church, among them the painter Titian (d 1576), whose 19th-century tomb occupies the second altar on the right (south) wall. Opposite, on the left wall, stands the *Monumento al Canova* (1827), an unmistakable marble pyramid that contains the sculptor's heart. To its right lies the wonderfully kitsch tomb of Doge Giovanni Pesaro (d 1659). The composer Claudio Monteverdi (d 1643) is buried in the third chapel to the left of the high altar.

Art The Frari's most striking painting is Titian's *Assumption* (1516–18), its position above the high altar designed to attract your attention from most of the church. The same painter's influential *Madonna di Ca' Pesaro* (1526), on the last altar of the left aisle, is almost equally captivating. The most beautiful work of art in the church, however, is Giovanni Bellini's sublime triptych of the *Madonna and Child between Sts Nicholas, Peter, Mark and Benedict* (1488), located in the sacristy off the right transept. In the first chapel on the right of the high altar is Donatello's statue of *St John the Baptist* (1438), the only work in Venice by the famous Florentine sculptor.

CA' REZZONICO

Gazing at the Grand Canal's palaces from a boat you can't help but wish you could see inside some of them, which is the attraction of Ca' Rezzonico, a museum that re-creates a Venetian palace as it might have appeared in the 18th century.

Palace The Ca' Rezzonico was begun in 1667 by Baldassare Longhena, one of the leading architects of his day, but remained half-finished following the ruin of its owner, Filippo Bon. In 1751 the shell was bought by the Rezzonico family, a *nouveau riche* clan, and then passed through several hands, including the son of poet Robert Browning, before opening as a museum in 1936. It begins in fine style with a sumptuous ballroom decorated with *trompe-l'œil* and enormous chandeliers. Highlights of subsequent rooms include ceiling frescoes by G B Tiepolo, some fine lacquerwork, Flemish tapestries and pastel portraits by Rosalba Carriera.

Paintings Much of the palace's second floor is devoted to a picture gallery, whose highlight is a pair of paintings by Canaletto, two of only a handful that remain on public display in Venice. Also of interest are Francesco Guardi's views of the city's convents and gambling rooms, together with 34 amateurish but fascinating portraits of Venetian life by Pietro Longhi, among them his well-known *Rhinoceros*, painted during the animal's stay in Venice in 1779. Rooms off to the right include a splendid bedchamber, complete with 18th-century closet and sponge-bag. The floor's final rooms contain the museum's pictorial high point, a series of satirical frescoes (1793–7) by G D Tiepolo. The third floor offers puppets, a reconstructed 18th-century pharmacy and fine views.

HIGHLIGHTS

- Ballroom
- G B Tiepolo ceiling frescoes
- Carriera portraits
- Lacquerwork
- Gondola cabin, or *felze* (ground floor)
- Canaletto paintings
- Francesco Guardi paintings
- Pietro Longhi paintings
- Bedchamber
- G D Tiepolo satirical frescoes

INFORMATION

- ✚ E12
- ✉ Fondamenta Rezzonico
- ☎ 041 241 0100/8506
- 🕐 Apr–Sep: Sat–Thu 9–5. Oct–Mar: Sat–Thu 10–4
- 🍴 Campo San Barnaba
- 🚤 Ca' Rezzonico 1
- ♿ Poor: steps to upper floors
- 💰 Expensive
- ↔ San Sebastiano (➤ 25), Scuola Grande dei Carmini (➤ 26), Scuola Grande di San Rocco (➤ 27), Santa Maria Gloriosa dei Frari (➤ 28), Gallerie dell'Accademia (➤ 31), Collezione Peggy Guggenheim (➤ 32)

A gondola cabin, or felze

SANTO STEFANO

HIGHLIGHTS

- Portal statues,
  Bartolomeo Bon
- Ceiling
- Tomb of Doge Morosini
- Tomb of Giovanni Gabriele
  (*d*1612), first altar on left
- *Monument to Giacomo
  Surian*, Pietro Lombardo
- *Madonna and Child with
  Saints*, Bonifaccio
- *Saints*, Bartolomeo Vivarini
- Tintoretto paintings
- *Monument to Giovanni Falier*
  (1808), Antonio Canova
  (baptistery)

INFORMATION

- ✚ F12
- ✉ Campo Santo Stefano (Campo
  Francesco Morosini)
- ☎ 041 522 5061 or 041 275
  0426
- 🕐 Mon–Sat 10–5:30; Sun
  3–5:30 (winter 1–5:30)
- 🍴 Campo Santo Stefano (Campo
  Francesco Morosini)
- 🚢 San Samuele or Sant'Angelo
  1, 3, 4, 82
- ♿ Very good
- 💰 Cheap
- ↔ Piazza San Marco
  (➤ 36), Museo Civico
  Correr (➤ 37)
- ❓ Catch the *traghetto* to
  San Tomà for quick
  access to sights on
  ➤ 25–29, 31 and 32

*The leaning
bell-tower of
Santo Stefano*

*Savour the sensation of walking from the
heat and bustle of a city into a building
which induces immediate calm, an effect
that is soon gained by the soothing Gothic
interior of Santo Stefano, one of Venice's
loveliest churches.*

Church Santo Stefano sits on the edge of Campo
Santo Stefano (also known as Campo Francesco
Morosini), one of Venice's most charming
squares; the nearby Paolin is an ideal place to sit
with a drink or ice cream (➤ 75). The church
itself has not always been so peaceful, having
been reconsecrated six times to wash away the
stain of blood spilled within its walls. Today, its
calm interior is overarched by an exquisite
'ship's keel' ceiling and framed by tie beams and
pillars of Greek and red Veronese marble.

Tombs At the centre of the nave lies Doge
Francesco Morosini (*d*1612, and buried under
Venice's largest tomb slab), famous for recaptur-
ing the Peloponnese and blowing up the
Parthenon with a single shot. Other tombs
command attention, notably Pietro Lombardo's
Monument to Giacomo Surian (*d*1493) on the wall
to the right of the main door,
but the church's chief artistic
interest lies in the gloomy
sacristy at the end of the right
nave. The altar wall features
two narrow-framed *Saints* by
Bartolomeo Vivarini, as well
as a recessed 13th-century
Byzantine icon. On the walls
to either side are four paintings by Tintoretto and four
portraits of Augustinian cardi-
nals (Santo Stefano is an
Augustinian church).

GALLERIE DELL'ACCADEMIA

An art gallery is almost superfluous in a city where art awaits you at every turn, but you would be missing out on a key Venetian experience without a trip to the Accademia, home to the world's greatest collection of Venetian paintings.

History The Accademia began life as Venice's art school in 1750, moving to its present site in 1807 when it garnered much of its permanent collection from churches and religious houses suppressed by Napoleonic decree. Its paintings, arranged chronologically, spread across 24 rooms.

Paintings Some of the gallery's best-known paintings are found in the first five rooms, Room 1 opening with Byzantine works, a style that influenced the city's earliest painters. Rooms 2 to 5 contain canvases by Carpaccio, Mantegna, Bellini and others, reflecting Venice's Renaissance heyday, as well as the Accademia's most famous painting, Giorgione's mysterious *Tempest*. Rooms 10 and 11 feature High Renaissance masterpieces, including Veronese's luxuriant *Supper in the House of Levi* and Tintoretto's iconoclastic *Miracle of the Slave* and *The Translation of the Body of St Mark*.

Cycles Leave plenty of time for the Accademia's highlights, two *storie*, or fresco cycles (rooms 20 and 21). The first, 'The Miracles of the True Cross' (1494–1510), was painted by a variety of artists for the Scuola di San Giovanni Evangelista. Each describes a miracle worked by a relic of the 'True Cross' owned by the *scuola*, though often the miracle itself takes second place to the fascinating anecdotal detail. The same is true for the second cycle, painted by Carpaccio for the Scuola di Sant'Orsola, with episodes from the 'Life of St Ursula'.

HIGHLIGHTS

- *Coronation of the Virgin* (c1345), Paolo Veneziano (Room 1)
- *Presentation of Jesus in the Temple*, Carpaccio (Room 2)
- *Madonna and Saints* (c1485), Giovanni Bellini (Room 2)
- *Tempest* (c1500), Giorgione (Room 5)
- *Supper in the House of Levi* (1573), Veronese (Room 10)
- *The Translation of the Body of St Mark* (c1560), Tintoretto (Room 10)
- *Pietà* (c1576), Titian (Room 10)
- Pietro Longhi paintings (Room 17)
- 'The Miracles of the True Cross' (Room 20)
- 'Life of St Ursula' (c1490–6), Carpaccio (Room 21)

INFORMATION

- ✚ E13
- ✉ Campo della Carità
- ☎ 041 522 2247
- 🕐 Mon–Sat 9–7; Sun 9–2
- 🍴 Campo Santo Stefano (Campo Francesco Morosini)
- 🚤 Accademia 1, 3, 4, 82
- ♿ Poor: some steps
- 💷 Very expensive
- ↔ Santo Stefano (➤ 30), Collezione Peggy Guggenheim (➤ 32), Santa Maria della Salute (➤ 34)
- ❓ Arrive early to avoid queues, especially on Sun

COLLEZIONE PEGGY GUGGENHEIM

HIGHLIGHTS

- Garden
- The New Wing
- Henry Moore sculptures
- *Bird in Space*, Constantin Brancusi
- *Red Tower*, De Chirico
- *Robing of the Bride*, Max Ernst
- Silver bedhead, Alexander Calder
- Jackson Pollock paintings
- *The Poet*, Pablo Picasso
- *Angel of the Citadel*, Marino Marini

INFORMATION

- 🕇 F13
- ✉ Palazzo Venier dei Leoni, Calle San Cristoforo
- ☎ 041 520 6288
- 🕐 Wed–Mon 11–6
- 🚢 Salute 1
- ♿ Good
- 💲 Expensive
- ↔ Ca' Rezzonico
  (➤ 29), Santo Stefano
  (➤ 30), Gallerie dell'Accademia
  (➤ 31), Santa Maria della Salute (➤ 34)

Its rather apt that the Accademia and Guggenheim, Venice's two most visited galleries, should be so close together, juxtaposing two matchless collections of paintings and sculptures – one traditional and one modern.

Palace The Guggenheim's small but polished collection was accumulated by Peggy Guggenheim (1898–1979), daughter of an American copper magnate, and installed by her in the 18th-century Palazzo Venier dei Leoni. The collection's appeal owes much to its immaculate presentation as well as to the beauty of its setting, many of the sculptures being arranged in a lovely garden. This has works by Henry Moore, Paolozzi, Giacometti and others, and houses the New Wing and appealing 'Museum Store'.

Gallery Guggenheim's taste and money allowed her to select high-quality works from virtually every modern-art movement of the 20th century. At the same time she had a penchant for the surreal and avant-garde, having enjoyed a brief relationship with the Surrealist painter Max Ernst. The collection features Cubist works by Picasso and Braque, and the Surrealism of Dalí, Magritte and Mirò. American modernists include Jackson Pollock, de Kooning and Rothko, while the English are represented by Francis Bacon. There are also sculptures by Calder and Brancusi, as well as works by Italians, notably the Futurists Balla and Boccioni. The most memorable work, however, is Marino Marini's provocative *Angel of the Citadel*, on the terrace overlooking the Grand Canal.

'Angel of the Citadel

10

MADONNA DELL'ORTO

*Madonna dell'Orto ranks high among the
many superb Venetian churches, its lovely
setting (well off the tourist trail) and
graceful red–brick façade complemented by
an airy interior that is filled with appealing works of art.*

Exterior The first church on the present site was
founded in 1350 and dedicated to St Christopher,
a statue of whom still dominates the lovely brick
and marble façade. The sculpture was commissioned by the Merchants' Guild, whose altar to
the saint (their patron) lay within the church. The
building was rededicated to the Virgin in 1377, an
act that was inspired by a miracle-working statue
of the Madonna found in a nearby vegetable
garden (*orto*). The elegant doorway, by
Bartolomeo Bon, is a Renaissance-tinged work
that departs from the façade's predominantly
Gothic inspiration. Note the onion dome of the
campanile, clear witness to the Byzantine
influence on Venetian architecture.

Interior The interior's artistic highlights begin
above the first altar on the right, which features
Cima da Conegliano's *St John the Baptist* (1493). At
the end of the right nave, above the door, stands
Tintoretto's dramatic *Presentation of the Virgin*
(1551). In the chapel to the right of the choir lies
Tintoretto's tomb, together with those of his children, Domenico and Marietta, both painters
themselves (Madonna dell'Orto was the family's
parish church). A wall separates the artist from
two of his finest paintings, the choir's grand *Last
Judgement* and *The Making of the Golden Calf*. Of the
three paintings in the apse to the rear, those on
the right and left – the *Beheading of St Paul* and *St
Peter's Vision of the Cross* – are by Tintoretto; the
central *Annunciation* is by Palma il Giovane. Four
of the five *Virtues* above are also by Tintoretto.

- Façade
- Doorway
- *St Christopher*, Nicolò di Giovanni
- Campanile
- *St John the Baptist*, Cima da Conegliano
- *Presentation of the Virgin*, Tintoretto
- *The Making of the Golden Calf*, Tintoretto
- *Last Judgement*, Tintoretto
- *St Agnes Raising Licinius*, Tintoretto (Cappella Contarini)

INFORMATION

- F8–9
- Campo Madonna dell'Orto
- 041 719933 or 041 275 0462
- Mon–Sat 10–5:30; Sun 3–5:30
- Madonna dell'Orto 52
- Good
- Cheap
- Ca' d'Oro (➤ 35), Campo dei Mori (➤ 54)

*Red-brick façade of the
Madonna dell'Orto*

33

11

SANTA MARIA DELLA SALUTE

HIGHLIGHTS

- Exterior
- Marble floor
- *Descent of the Holy Spirit*, Titian
- *The Virgin Casting out the Plague*, Juste le Court
- *Feast at Cana* (1561), Tintoretto (sacristy)
- *Cain and Abel* (1542–4), Titian (sacristy)
- *David and Goliath* (1542–4), Titian (sacristy)
- *Sacrifice of Abraham* (1542–4), Titian (sacristy)
- *St Mark Enthroned between Sts Cosmas, Damian, Roch and Sebastian* (1510), Titian (sacristy)
- *Madonna*, Palma il Vecchio

INFORMATION

- ✚ F13
- ✉ Campo della Salute
- ☎ 041 522 5558
- ⏰ Daily 9–noon, 3–5:30
- 🚢 Salute 1
- ♿ Poor: several steps
- 🎟 Church free. Sacristy cheap
- ↔ Ca' Rezzonico (➤ 29), Santo Stefano (➤ 30), Gallerie dell'Accademia (➤ 31), Collezione Peggy Guggenheim (➤ 32)

The Salute's interior

In a city where almost every street and canal offers a memorable vista, the church of Santa Maria della Salute, proudly situated at the entrance to the Grand Canal, forms part of the panorama most people readily associate with Venice.

Plague In 1630 Venice found itself ravaged by a plague so severe that the Senate promised to build a church in honour of the Virgin if she could save the city. Within weeks the pestilence had abated, and on 1 April the following year the first stone of the Salute, meaning 'health' and 'salvation' in Italian, was laid. Its architect, chosen after a competition, was Baldassare Longhena, responsible for a host of outstanding Venetian buildings. His design proved to be a baroque model for years to come, combining the Palladian influence of his master, Scamozzi (Palladio's closest follower), with a range of personal innovations.

Interior The Salute's main impact is as a distant prospect, its dazzling exterior detail and great dome (modelled on that of St Peter's in Rome) forming irreplaceable elements of the Venetian skyline. The church's interior is more restrained, its fine marble floor being the first thing that catches your eye. Moving left from the side entrance, the third of the three altars boasts an early painting by Titian, the *Descent of the Holy Spirit* (1550). The high altar supports *The Virgin Casting out the Plague* (1670), a magnificent sculpture designed by Longhena and carved by Juste le Court. The supplicant figure on the left represents Venice, while the elderly harridan moving off to the right symbolises the plague. It is well worth paying the entrance fee for the sacristy, which contains paintings by Titian and Tintoretto.

CA' D'ORO

The smaller and less-famous galleries of a city are often more rewarding than some of the bigger attractions. The Ca' d'Oro is no exception, its collection of paintings, sculptures and objets d'art being one of the most absorbing in Venice.

Palace The Ca' d'Oro, or 'House of Gold', takes its name from the gilding that once covered its façade, a decorative veneer now worn away by wind and rain. The façade remains one of the most accomplished pieces of Venetian-Byzantine architecture in the city.

The same, sadly, cannot be said of the interior, which has been ravaged by a succession of hapless owners. The palace was handed over to the state in 1916.

Gallery The gallery divides into two floors, each of these arranged around a central *portego* (see panel ➤ 57). On the first floor a captivating polyptych of the *Crucifixion* by Antonio Vivarini greets you, along with sculptural fragments belonging to the *Massacre of the Innocents* (14th century). Moving right you come to the gallery's pictorial masterpiece, Mantegna's sombre *St Sebastian* (1506). To its left, in the *portego*, is a pair of busts by Tullio Lombardo (15th century), followed by six bronze reliefs by Andrea Briscio (1470–1532). Rooms off the *portego* contain medallions, a *Madonna* by Giovanni Bellini, and Florentine and Sienese paintings. Upstairs are tapestries, paintings by Titian, Van Dyck and Tintoretto, and damaged frescoes by Pordenone, Titian and Giorgione.

HIGHLIGHTS

- Grand Canal façade
- *Massacre of the Innocents*, artist unknown
- *Crucifixion*, Antonio Vivarini
- Three-dimensional *paliotto* with *Scenes from the Life of St Catherine* (16th century), artist unknown
- *St Sebastian*, Andrea Mantegna
- *Man* and *Woman*, busts by Tullio Lombardo
- *The Story of the True Cross*, bronze reliefs by Andrea Briscio
- *Madonna of the Beautiful Eyes*, Giovanni Bellini
- *Flagellation*, Luca Signorelli
- *Scenes from the Life of Lucrezia*, Biagio d'Antonio

The Ca' d'Oro's ornate façade

INFORMATION

13

PIAZZA SAN MARCO

Avoid visiting Piazza San Marco on your first morning as the crowds might turn you against Venice for good. Once you've acquired a taste for the city you'll be ready to venture into one of the world's most famous squares.

Hordes Europe's 'drawing-room' was how Napoleon described Venice's main square, though glancing at its present-day summer crowds he would probably be less complimentary. The piazza is too crowded, but early in the morning or off-season its considerable charms can still work their spell. The area was initially planted with an orchard belonging to the nuns of nearby San Zaccaria. Before the building of the Basilica, Campanile and Palazzo Ducale – the square's most famous sights – it was home to a lighthouse and a pair of churches. Its 1,000-year transformation began in the 9th century, when the nuns sacrificed their trees to make way for the Basilica and Palazzo Ducale. The 12th century saw the arrival of the Procuratie, built to house Venice's civil servants, followed in the 16th century by the Zecca (Mint) and Libreria Sansoviniana.

Sights Over and above the obvious sights and famous cafés, make a point of seeing the archaeological museum, the Torre dell'Orologio (1496–9), complete with zodiac and 24-hour clock-face, and the two granite columns that stand on the waterfront area in front of the Palazzo Ducale. One is topped with the lion of St Mark, the other with St Theodore and a beast of mysterious origin. The area was once a place of execution, hence it is considered unlucky to walk between the pillars. The Libreria Sansoviniana, designed by Sansovino, was considered one of the greatest buildings of its day – despite the fact that its ceiling came crashing down shortly after completion.

HIGHLIGHTS

- Basilica di San Marco
- Palazzo Ducale
- Campanile
- Museo Civico Correr
- Procuratie
- Libreria Sansoviniana
- Torre dell'Orologio
- Zecca
- Columns
- Florian

INFORMATION

MUSEO CIVICO CORRER

Probably only a fraction of the visitors thronging Piazza San Marco venture into the Museo Civico Correr. Those who do not are missing not only Venice's finest museum, but also a picture gallery with a remarkable collection of paintings.

History Much of the Correr's collection was accumulated by Abbot Teodoro Correr, a Venetian worthy, and bequeathed to the city in 1830. Today, it spreads over three floors, devoted respectively to historical displays, an art gallery and the small Museo del Risorgimento (this details the 19th-century unification of Italy). The opening rooms feature lovely old prints and paintings of the city, followed by salons devoted to different episodes of Venetian history. Particularly outstanding are the costumes and hats, standards, armour, globes, old weapons and ships' instruments exibits. Perhaps the most memorable section, however, is the footwear display showing the famous 'platform' shoes once worn by Venetian ladies of rank.

Art The last section of the first floor consists of a large hall devoted to several fine sculptures by Antonio Canova. Look out, in particular, for the touching study of Daedalus fixing a pair of flimsy wings to Icarus's arms. Occupying the second floor is the city's second-finest art gallery after the Accademia. Its most popular picture is Carpaccio's *Two Women* (1507), a masterful study of ennui that was for many years known as *The Courtesans* after its protagonists' plunging necklines. Other well-known paintings include *The Man in the Red Hat* (by either Carpaccio or Lorenzo Lotto) and a *Pietà* by Antonello da Messina, together with works by Cosmè Tura, Alvise Vivarini, and Jacopo, Giovanni and Gentile Bellini.

HIGHLIGHTS

- Aerial view of Venice (1500), Jacopo de' Barbari
- Daedalus and Icarus, Canova
- Two Women, Carpaccio
- The Man in the Red Hat, Lorenzo Lotto (attributed)
- Pietà, Antonello da Messina
- Madonna and Child, Giovanni Bellini

Gentile Bellini's Doge Giovanni Mocenigo

INFORMATION

- G12
- ✉ Procuratie Nuove, Ala Napoleonica, Piazza San Marco
- ☎ 041 522 5625
- 🕐 Apr–Oct: daily 9–7. Nov–Mar: daily 9–5
- 🍴 Piazza San Marco
- 🚏 San Marco 1, 3, 4, 82
- ♿ Poor
- 💲 Expensive (joint ticket with Palazzo Ducale)
- ↔ Piazza San Marco (➤ 36), Campanile (➤ 38), Basilica di San Marco (➤ 39)

CAMPANILE

One look at the queues might be enough to put you off taking the lift up the Campanile, but you should grit your teeth and wait in line, for the views from the top – which stretch to the Alps on a clear day – are absolutely unforgettable.

Purpose Venice's tallest building (98.5m) was reputedly founded in 912 on 25 April, the feast day of St Mark. In its earliest role it served as a bell tower for the Basilica and as a lighthouse for the harbour below. Its summit was sheathed in bronze, designed to catch the sun's rays and act as a beacon during the day. Venetians had long trusted the Campanile's supposedly massive foundations, believed to fan out in a star-shaped bulwark below the piazza. In fact, they were just 20m deep, a design fault exacerbated over the centuries by wind, rain and salt-water erosion, not to mention countless lightning strikes.

Collapse Disaster struck on 14 July 1902, when, after a few warning cracks, the 990-year-old Campanile collapsed gently to the ground in front of a bewildered crowd. Remarkably no one was hurt – the only casualty being the keeper's cat, which had returned to the evacuated tower to finish its breakfast. More remarkable still, the Basilica and Palazzo Ducale escaped virtually unscathed. Plans were immediately made to rebuild the tower *dov' era e com' era* – 'where it was and how it was'. The new Campanile was inaugurated on 25 April 1912, exactly 1,000 years after its predecessor – though this time 600 tonnes lighter and with an extra 1,000 foundation piles.

BASILICA DI SAN MARCO

Don't allow yourself to be discouraged by the teeming crowds that engulf the Basilica di San Marco, as ultimately no one can fail to remain unimpressed by what is surely one of the world's greatest medieval buildings.

Chapel The Basilica was begun in 832 to house the body of St Mark, stolen from Alexandria by Venetian merchants four years earlier. For almost a thousand years it served as the doge's private 'chapel' and the city's spiritual heart, accumulating the decorative fruits of a millennium to emerge as the most exotic hybrid of Western and Byzantine architecture in Europe. The original building (destroyed by rioting) was replaced in 978 and again in 1094, the church from the latter date being mostly the one you see today.

Exploring Admiring the Basilica's treasures is exhausting, partly because there are so many, and partly because the almost constant crowds make exploring a dispiriting business. This said, the building is still overwhelmingly striking, though you should spend a few minutes taking in some of the exterior details before plunging inside. These include the *Translation of the Body of St Mark to the Basilica* (1260–70) above the leftmost door, the west façade's only original mosaic (the rest are later copies), and the superb Romanesque carvings (1240–65) above the central door. Inside, you should see the famous bronze horses (probably 3rd century AD) in the Museo Marciano, the view from the Loggia dei Cavalli, the treasury (full of antique silverware) and the magnificent Pala d'Oro, an altar screen encrusted with over 2,600 pearls, rubies, emeralds and other precious stones.

HIGHLIGHTS

- ● Central door
- ● Façade mosaics
- ● Bronze horses
- ● View from Loggia dei Cavalli
- ● Rood screen
- ● Mosaic pavement
- ● Treasury
- ● Madonna de Nicopeia
- ● Pala d'Oro
- ● Interior mosaics

INFORMATION

- ✚ G12–H12
- ✉ Piazza San Marco
- ☎ 041 522 5205/5697
- ◷ Summer: Mon–Sat 9:45–5; Sun 2–5. Winter: Mon–Sat 9:45–4; Sun 2–4
- 🍴 Piazza San Marco
- 🚌 San Marco or San Zaccaria 1, 3, 4, 52, 82
- ♿ Some steps; uneven floors
- 🏛 Basilica free. Museo Marciano cheap. Treasury cheap. Pala d'Oro cheap
- ↔ Piazza San Marco (➤ 36), Museo Civico Correr (➤ 37), Campanile (➤ 38), Palazzo Ducale (➤ 40)

St Mark's richly decorated façade

39

17

PALAZZO DUCALE

Italy has a host of beautiful Gothic buildings, but the Palazzo Ducale is the most captivating: the ornate and many-roomed seat of the doge and home to Venice's various offices of state for almost a thousand years.

History The first ducal palace, completed in 814, was a severe fortress built on one of the few clay redoubts in the lagoon. This burned down in 976, as did its successor in 1106. By 1419 the palace was in its third – and more or less final – incarnation. Three years later, the great hall, or Sala del Maggior Consiglio, was completed – one of many additions made to the interior as the machinery of the state expanded. By 1550 most work had been completed, only to be undone by fires in 1574 and 1577, conflagrations which not only destroyed masterpieces by some of Venice's greatest painters, but also threatened the entire building with collapse. Restoration work continued on and off until the 1880s.

Details Outside, note the famous Ponte dei Sospiri (Bridge of Sighs), tucked down a canal at the palace's eastern end, and the fine sculptures on each of the building's three corners. Also take in the excellent carving of the pillars and capitals, and the palace's superb main doorway, the Porta della Carta (1438–43), together with the famous little group of red porphyry knights, or tetrarchs, to its left. Beyond the courtyard and ticket office an ornate staircase leads up several flights to the beginning of the palace's set itinerary, a marked route that leads you from one lavishly decorated room to the next. Look out for works by Tintoretto, Veronese and other Venetian masters, in particular Tintoretto's gargantuan *Paradiso* (1588–92), the world's largest oil painting, in the Sala del Maggior Consiglio.

HIGHLIGHTS

- Bridge of Sighs
- Tetrarchs
- Porta della Carta
- Scala dei Giganti
- Arco Foscari
- Sala dell'Anticollegio
- Sala del Collegio
- Sala del Maggior Consiglio
- Armoury
- Prisons

INFORMATION

➕ H12

✉ Piazzetta San Marco

☎ Palace 041 522 4951. Guided tours 041 520 4287

🕐 Palace Apr–Oct: 9–7 (last ticket sold 5:30). Nov–Mar: 9–5 (last ticket sold 3:30). Guided tours 2–3 per morning daily

🍴 Piazza San Marco

🚤 San Marco or San Zaccaria 1, 3, 4, 52, 82

♿ Poor: stairs to upper floors

💰 Expensive (joint ticket with Muso Civico Correr)

↔ Museo Civico Correr (➤ 37), Campanile (➤ 38), Basilica di San Marco (➤ 39)

Bridge of Sighs

SANTA MARIA DEI MIRACOLI

A visitor soon gets used to being brought up short in Venice by surprises and unexpected views around almost every corner, but none quite compares with a first glimpse of the beautiful multi-coloured marbles of Santa Maria dei Miracoli.

Miracles The church was built to house an image of the Virgin, painted in 1409 and originally intended to be placed on the outside of a house (a common practice in Venice). Miracles (*miracoli*) began to be associated with the image in 1480, leading to a flood of votive donations, which allowed the authorities to commission a church for the icon from Pietro Lombardo. One of the leading architects of his day, Lombardo created a building that relied for its effect almost entirely on colour, embellishing his church in a variety of honey-coloured marbles, porphyry panels and serpentine inlays: legend has it that the decorations consisted of left-over materials from the Basilica. A moat-like canal enhances the charm, providing a shimmering mirror for the multi-hued marbles.

Interior Lombardo's innovative use of marble continues inside, which is filled with an array of sculptures that were executed in tandem with his sons, Tullio and Antonio. The best is the carving on the two pillars that support the nuns' choir (near the entrance); on the half-figures of the balustrade fronting the raised choir; among the exotica at the base of the choir's pillars. The striking ceiling is decorated with 50 *Saints and Prophets* (1528), the work of Pier Pennacchi. Nicolò di Pietro's *Madonna and Child*, the miraculous image for which the church was built, adorns the high altar.

HIGHLIGHTS

- Coloured marbles
- Decorative inlays
- False pillars
- Bas-reliefs
- Nuns' choir
- Balustrade
- Pillar carving
- Raised choir
- *Madonna and Child*, Nicolò di Pietro
- Ceiling

Façade detail

INFORMATION

- 🟦 G11
- ✉ Campo dei Miracoli
- ☎ 041 528 3903 or 041 275 0462
- 🕐 Mon–Sat 10–5:30; Sun 3–5:30
- 🍴 Campo Santa Maria Nova
- 🚤 Rialto 1, 3, 82
- ♿ Good: few steps
- 💰 Cheap
- ↔ Santa Maria Formosa (➤ 42), Santi Giovanni e Paolo (➤ 43)

SANTA MARIA FORMOSA

HIGHLIGHTS

- Façades
- Martial bas-reliefs
- Plaque recording 1916 incendiary bomb
- Campanile's stone mask
- Interior
- *Madonna della Misericordia,* Bartolomeo Vivarini
- *Santa Barbara,* Palma il Vecchio

INFORMATION

- ✚ H11
- ✉ Campo Santa Maria Formosa
- ☎ 041 275 0462
- ◷ Mon–Sat 10–5:30; Sun 3–5:30
- 🍴 Campo Santa Maria Formosa
- 🚇 Rialto or Fondamente Nuove 1, 52, 82
- ♿ Good
- 👍 Cheap
- ↔ Piazza San Marco (➤ 36), Basilica di San Marco (➤ 39), Palazzo Ducale (➤ 40), Santa Maria dei Miracoli (➤ 41), Santi Giovanni e Paolo (➤ 43), Campo Santa Maria Formosa (➤ 55)

Santa Maria Formosa's appeal rests partly on its surrounding square, Campo Santa Maria Formosa. An archetypal Venetian square, it is a pleasantly rambling affair, full of local colour and lined with attractive cafés and palaces.

Exterior This church takes its name from *una Madonna formosa*, a 'buxom Madonna', which appeared to St Magno in the 7th century and instructed him to follow a small white cloud and build a church wherever it settled. The present building, completed in 1492, was grafted onto an 11th-century Byzantine church, from which it borrowed its Greek-cross plan, a common feature of Byzantine (and later) churches dedicated to the Virgin. The façade (1542) was paid for by the Cappello family, hence its statue of Vincenzo Cappello, a Venetian admiral. Note the carved face on the bell tower to the left, one of Venice's most famous grotesques.

Interior The church's interior is a unique blend of Renaissance decoration and ersatz Byzantine cupolas, barrel vaults and narrow-columned screens. Of particular interest are two paintings, the first being Bartolomeo Vivarini's *Madonna della Misericordia* (1473), a triptych in the first chapel on the right (south) side. It was financed by the church's congregation, depicted in the picture sheltering beneath the Virgin's protective cloak. The second and more famous picture, Palma il Vecchio's *Santa Barbara* (1522–4), reveals the artist's daughter as its model. Barbara was martyred by her own father, who was then struck down by lightning, a death-dealing blow from the heavens that made Barbara the patron saint of artillerymen – hence the cannon at the base of the painting and the cannon-balls strewn around the chapel floor.

SANTI GIOVANNI E PAOLO

Nowhere in Venice is there a greater collection of superb sculpture under one roof than in Santi Giovanni e Paolo, a majestic Gothic church whose walls are lined with the funerary monuments of more than 20 of the city's doges.

Church Santi Giovanni e Paolo, known locally as San Zanipolo, is rivalled only by Santa Maria Gloriosa dei Frari (▶ 28). Its appeal rests on a handful of superb paintings, its tremendous tombs and on surroundings that include the magnificent façade of the adjacent Scuola Grande di San Marco and Verrocchio's great equestrian statue of Bartolomeo Colleoni (▶ 54). The church was begun in 1246 by Doge Giacomo Tiepolo, who is buried in the most ornate of the four wall tombs built into the façade. Inside, further tombs lie ranged around the walls, many by some of Venice's finest medieval sculptors. The best include the monuments to Doge Pietro Mocenigo (*d*1476) by Pietro, Tullio and Antonio Lombardo (left of the main door), and to Doge Michele Morosini (*d*1382), on the wall to the right of the high altar.

Paintings The most outstanding of the church's paintings are Giovanni Bellini's beautiful and recently restored polyptych of *St Vincent Ferrer* (second altar on the right) and the works in the south transept, which include *The Coronation of the Virgin*, attributed to Cima da Conegliano, and Lorenzo Lotto's wonderful *St Antonino Pierozzi Giving Alms to the Poor* (1542).

HIGHLIGHTS

- Main portal
- *Monument to Doge Pietro Mocenigo*, Pietro Lombardo
- *St Vincent Ferrer* (1465), Giovanni Bellini
- Cappella della Madonna della Pace
- *St Antonius Pierozzi Giving Alms to the Poor*, Lorenzo Lotto
- *Monument to Doge Michele Morosini*
- *Monument to Doge Andrea Vendramin* (*d*1478)
- *Monument to Doge Marco Corner* (*d*1368), Nino Pisano
- Veronese ceiling paintings, Cappella del Rosario
- *Monument to Doge Nicolò Marcello*, Pietro Lombardo

INFORMATION

✚ H11
✉ Campo Santi Giovanni e Paolo
☎ 041 523 5913
🕐 Daily 7:30–12:30, 3–7:30
🍴 Campo Santi Giovanni e Paolo
🚢 Fondamente Nuove or Ospedale Civile 12, 13, 52
♿ Good: one step
🆓 Free
↔ Santa Maria dei Miracoli (▶ 41), Santa Maria Formosa (▶ 42)

Monument to Doge Pietro Mocenigo

SAN GIORGIO MAGGIORE

INFORMATION

The outlook from the top of the Campanile is spell-binding, but for a superb view of the lagoon and back to San Marco and the city, go up the bell tower of San Giorgio Maggiore, a magnificent Palladian church near the Giudecca.

Classical The church's dazzling marble façade provides one of the great architectural set pieces of the Venetian skyline. Founded in 790, the first church on the site was destroyed by an earthquake in 1223, together with an adjoining Benedictine monastery built in 982. While the monastery was rebuilt in 1443, the church had to wait until 1559 and the arrival of the great Vicenzan architect, Andrea Palladio. His design for the new church adopted many of the architectural idioms of the ancient world (notably the majestic four-columned portico) to produce one of Italy's most beautiful neoclassical buildings.

Interior The ancient world also influenced the sparse interior, where light is introduced by high windows, a device borrowed from the bathhouses of 3rd-century Rome. The major works of art are Jacopo Bassano's famous *Adoration of the Shepherds* (1582), located above the second altar on the right, and a pair of outstanding paintings by Tintoretto – *The Fall of Manna* (1594) and *The Last Supper* (1594) – located on the walls of the chancel. Also worth a look is the church's choir (1594–8), tucked away behind the high altar. Few of the stalls, which depict *Scenes from the Life of St Benedict*, have much in the way of individual delicacy, but their carving and overall effect are impressive. All else in the church pales, however, alongside the breathtaking view from the campanile, reached by a lift at the end of the north aisle.

Carved wood choir stalls inside San Giorgio Maggiore

SAN ZACCARIA

You'll never tire of visiting the church of San Zaccaria, a charming medley of Gothic and Renaissance architecture whose calm interior contains Giovanni Bellini's **Madonna and Child with Saints,** *one of Venice's most beautiful altarpieces.*

Changes San Zaccaria was founded in the 9th century, received a Romanesque veneer a century later, and was overhauled again in 1174. Rebuilding began again in the 14th century, when the church acquired a Gothic feel, though no sooner had it been completed than another new church was begun. Old and new versions are still visible, the brick façade of the earlier church on the right, the white marble front of the latter to its left. The newer façade is one of the most important in Venice, displaying a moment of architectural transition from Gothic to Renaissance. The Gothic lower half is by Antonio Gambello, while the Renaissance upper section (added on Gambello's death in 1481) is the work of Mauro Coducci.

Interior The nave's second altar contains Giovanni Bellini's delightful *Madonna and Child with Saints* (1505). Across the nave in the second altar on the right lie the relics of San Zaccaria (Zachery or Zaccharias), the father of John the Baptist. The 'museum' off the south aisle features two linked chapels, the first of which contains an early Tintoretto, *The Birth of John the Baptist* (above the main altar). Steps in the adjoining Cappella di San Tarasio lead down to a dank 9th-century crypt, final resting place of eight of the city's first doges. The chapel's vaults contain early Renaissance frescoes by Andrea del Castagno (1442), while the altars below feature three Gothic altarpieces by Antonio Vivarini.

HIGHLIGHTS

- Façade bas-reliefs (1440), Antonio Gambello
- Upper façade, Mauro Coducci
- *Madonna and Child with Saints*, Giovanni Bellini
- Tomb of Alessandro Vittoria (1595)
- Relics of San Zaccaria
- *The Birth of John the Baptist*, Tintoretto
- Crypt
- Vault frescoes, Andrea del Castagno
- Altarpieces, Antonio Vivarini and Giovanni d'Alemagna
- Predella, Paolo Veneziano

INFORMATION

- ✚ H12
- ✉ Campo di San Zaccaria
- ☎ 041 522 1257
- ◷ Daily 10–noon, 4–6
- 🍴 Campo San Provolo
- 🚤 San Zaccaria 1, 10, 20, 52, 82
- ♿ Good
- ⛪ Church free. Cappella di San Tarasio cheap
- ↔ Piazza San Marco (➤ 36), Basilica di San Marco (➤ 39), Palazzo Ducale (➤ 40), Scuola di San Giorgio degli Schiavoni (➤ 46), San Giovanni in Bragora (➤ 47)

23

SCUOLA DI SAN GIORGIO DEGLI SCHIAVONI

HIGHLIGHTS

- Ceiling
- St George Slaying the Dragon
- Triumph of St George
- St George Baptising the Gentiles
- The Miracle of St Tryphon
- The Agony in the Garden
- The Calling of St Matthew
- Miracle of the Lion
- The Funeral of St Jerome
- The Vision of St Augustine

INFORMATION

- ✚ J12
- ✉ Calle dei Furlani
- ☎ 041 522 8828
- 🕐 Apr–Oct: Tue–Sat 9:30–12:30, 3–6:30. Nov–Mar: Tue–Sat 10–12:30, 3–6; Sun mornings only
- 🍴 Fondamenta di San Lorenzo
- 🚆 San Zaccaria 1, 52, 82
- ♿ Good
- 🚽 Moderate
- ↔ San Zaccaria (➤ 45), San Giovanni in Bragora (➤ 47), Museo Storico Navale (➤ 48)

Admiring paintings in galleries is enjoyable, but to look at works of art in the buildings for which they were painted is an added bonus. This intimate scuola, *with its charming cycle of Carpaccio paintings, allows you to do just that.*

Slavs This tiny *scuola* (religious or charitable confraternity) was founded in 1451 to look after Venice's Dalmatian, or Slav (*Schiavoni*), population. Dalmatia, roughly present-day Croatia, was among the first territories absorbed by Venice (in the 9th century). By the 15th century the city had a large community of expatriate Dalmatian sailors, artisans and merchants. In 1502 Carpaccio was commissioned to decorate their humble *scuola* with scenes from the lives of Dalmatia's three patron saints: George, Tryphon and Jerome. On their completion (in 1508), the paintings were installed in the headquarters' upper gallery, only to be moved to their present position when the *scuola* was rebuilt in 1551.

Paintings Nine paintings, plus an altarpiece by Carpaccio's son, Benedetto, lie ranged around the walls under one of the loveliest ceilings imaginable. The cycle starts on the north wall with *St George Slaying the Dragon*, a wonderfully graphic painting which, like much of Carpaccio's work, is enlivened with a wealth of exotic and extraneous detail. Moving right you come to the *Triumph of St George, St George Baptising the Gentiles*, and *The Miracle of St Tryphon*, which depicts the obscure boy-saint exorcising a demon from the daughter of the Roman Emperor Gordian. The next two, *The Agony in the Garden* and *The Calling of St Matthew*, are followed by three works concerned with St Jerome: the best known is *The Vision of St Augustine*, in which Augustine is visited by a vision announcing Jerome's death.

SAN GIOVANNI IN BRAGORA

Choosing a favourite small Venetian church is no easy matter as there are so many contenders, but many lovers of the city would probably choose San Giovanni in Bragora, the baptismal church of the Venetian composer Antonio Vivaldi.

Names Founded in the 8th century, San Giovanni in Bragora is one of Venice's oldest churches, its name deriving either from *brágora*, meaning 'market-place'; from two dialect words, *brago* ('mud') and *gora* ('stagnant canal'); from the Greek *agora*, meaning 'town square'; from *bragolare* ('to fish'); or from the region in the Middle East which yielded the relics of St John the Baptist, to whom the church is dedicated. The Venetian composer Antonio Vivaldi was baptised here, and the original font, together with copies of the baptismal documents, stands at the beginning of the left nave.

Paintings The paintings in the lovely interior begin on the south wall to the left of the first chapel with a triptych by Francesco Bissolo and a *Madonna and Saints* by Bartolomeo Vivarini. Between these, above the confessional, stands a small Byzantine Madonna. A relief above the sacristy door is flanked on the left by Alvise Vivarini's *Risen Christ* (1498) and on the right by Cima da Conegliano's *Constantine and St Helena* (1502). Cima also painted the church's pictorial highlight, *The Baptism of Christ* (1494), its beautiful frame and ethereal blues offset by the high altar's stuccoed vaults. No less lovely are two paintings on the wall of the north aisle: a small *Head of the Saviour* by Alvise Vivarini; and Bartolomeo Vivarini's enchanting *Madonna and Child* (1478), to the right of the second chapel.

HIGHLIGHTS

- Façade
- Vivaldi's baptismal font
- *Madonna and Saints*, Bartolomeo Vivarini
- Byzantine Madonna
- Relics of St John the Almsgiver (second chapel on right)
- *Risen Christ*, Alvise Vivarini
- *Constantine and St Helena*, Cima da Conegliano
- *The Baptism of Christ*, Cima da Conegliano
- *Head of the Saviour*, Alvise Vivarini
- *Madonna and Child*, Bartolomeo Vivarini

INFORMATION

- ✠ J12
- ✉ Campo Bandiera e Moro
- ☎ 041 522 5906
- 🕐 Mon–Sat 8:30–11; Sun 3–5
- 🍴 Campo Bandiera e Moro
- 🚊 Arsenale or San Zaccaria 1
- ♿ Good
- 💲 Free
- ↔ San Zaccaria
- (➤ 45), Scuola di San Giorgio degli Schiavoni (➤ 46), Museo Storico

Vivaldi's baptismal font

25

MUSEO STORICO NAVALE

Model of the Bucintoro

INFORMATION

If you expected a dull and perfunctory museum, Venice's Museo Storico Navale is a revelation. Its enjoyably presented displays of maritime ephemera put Venice and the sea, its inseparable ally, into a clear historical context.

Boats The idea of a maritime museum originated in 1815 by the Austrians, who collected remnants of the Venetian Navy (dispersed and partly destroyed by Napoleon) and mixed them with scale models of Venetian vessels and other pieces of maritime ephemera. In 1958 the collection, swollen over the years, was moved to its present site close to the entrance to the Arsenale, the great shipyards which once produced the galleys that formed the cornerstone of Venice's far-flung empire. Before or after seeing the museum, it is well worth walking the short distance north to Campo Arsenale to admire the fine Renaissance gateway (1460) which marks the entrance to the yards (now in the hands of the Italian navy).

Museum The museum's four floors trace the history of the Venetian and Italian navies, illustrating their development with a succession of uniforms, medals, flags, pendants, maps, diagrams, cannon, mortars, machine-guns, and beautifully crafted scale models of forts and boats. Look out in particular for the models of the *triremi*, the oar-driven galleys that formed the core of the Venetian fleet, and for the displays on the third floor devoted to the gondola. The mezzanine has a shimmering collection of shells and an exhibit about the unexpectedly close links between the maritime traditions of Venice and Sweden. Be sure to visit the separate Padiglione delle Navi, a wonderful collection of gondolas, funeral barques and other lovely old boats housed in the Arsenale's former oarsmakers' sheds.

VENICE's *best*

PAINTINGS

The Miracle of the Cross at Ponte San Lorenzo by Gentile Bellini

Family portrait

Iacopo Pesaro, who commissioned Titian's *Madonna di Ca' Pesaro*, is depicted in the painting in front of the knight on the left (who may be a self-portrait of Titian). Pesaro led a fleet against the Turks in 1502, partly in response to a call from the Borgia pope, Alexander VI – hence the knight in armour behind Pesaro, whose standard bears the Pesaro and Borgia coats of arms. The same figure leads a turbanned Turk and black slave towards St Peter, a symbol of their conversion and of the Christian spirit of the campaign. On the right, St Francis holds his hands over Iacopo's brother, Francesco, while the boy looking out from the painting is Iacopo's nephew and heir, Lunardo. The face of the Madonna was modelled on Titian's wife, Celia, who died soon after in childbirth.

GENTILE BELLINI
The Miracle of the Cross at Ponte San Lorenzo (1500)
One of a cycle of paintings depicting 'The Miracles of the True Cross', this picture shows the head of the Scuola di San Giovanni Evangelista holding aloft a reliquary containing a fragment of the 'True Cross' (the reliquary had accidentally been dropped into a canal and floated miraculously to the surface).
Location Gallerie dell'Accademia (➤ 31)

GIOVANNI BELLINI
Madonna and Child between Sts Nicholas, Peter, Mark and Benedict (1488)
The effect of this painting is enhanced by the perspective used to place the Madonna in her gold-lined recess, and the manner in which the frame is designed to continue the painting's perspective scheme. The picture was a gift from Pietro (Peter) Pesaro and his sons Niccolò, Marco and Benedetto – hence the choice of saints depicted.
Location Santa Maria Gloriosa dei Frari (➤ 28)

VITTORE CARPACCIO
St George Slaying the Dragon (1502–8)
Note the remains of the dragon's earlier victims, depicted in grisly detail in the foreground of the painting, and the manner in which the saint's lance divides the picture into compositional 'triangles'. Each section has its own colour and narrative preoccupation: dragon and city, St George and Selene (the princess he has saved), the sky, and the human debris of the foreground.
Location Scuola di San Giorgio degli Schiavoni (➤ 46)

VITTORE CARPACCIO
Two Women (1507)
This picture was long thought to depict a pair of courtesans, though the distinctive hairstyles and plunging necklines of the dresses were typical of many women of the time.
Location Museo Civico Correr (➤ 37)

GIAN ANTONIO FUMIANI
The Miracles and Martyrdom of St Pantaleone (1704)
Although not artistically distinguished, this ceiling painting impresses by its sheer scale, its 60 linked panels forming the world's largest area of painted canvas.
Location San Pantalon (➤ 53)

JACOPO ROBUSTI TINTORETTO

Paradiso (1588–92)

At 140sq m this is the world's largest single oil painting. Painted free of charge when Tintoretto was in his seventies, it depicts the regiment of the saved as described in Canto XXX of Dante's *Paradiso*.

Location Palazzo Ducale (➤ 40)

JACOPO ROBUSTI TINTORETTO

Crucifixion (1565)

Victorian critic John Ruskin wrote of this painting: 'I must leave this picture to work its will on the spectator, for it is beyond all analysis and above all praise.' Novelist Henry James thought: 'Surely no single picture in the world contains more of human life…there is everything in it.'

Location Scuola Grande di San Rocco (➤ 27)

TIZIANO VECELLO TITIAN

Assumption (1516–18)

This powerful painting sits above the Frari's high altar, and is designed to attract your attention from most parts of the church. It was not always highly esteemed, having been criticised as too revolutionary by the Franciscans who commissioned it, and was kept in storage until earlier this century.

Location Santa Maria Gloriosa dei Frari (➤ 28)

TIZIANO VECELLO TITIAN

Madonna di Ca' Pesaro (1526)

This picture was commissioned in 1519 by Bishop Pesaro (see panel), who lies buried in a tomb to the right of the painting. Note the two columns that bisect the picture and the off-centre position of the Madonna, both interesting compositional devices.

Location Santa Maria Gloriosa dei Frari (➤ 28)

PAOLO VERONESE

Supper in the House of Levi (1573)

This picture was painted as a *Last Supper* for the refectory of Santi Giovanni e Paolo, but after complaints from the Inquisition – who objected to its 'buffoons, drunkards, Germans, dwarfs and similar indecencies' – Veronese changed its name (but not its content). Veronese himself is the figure in green, centre left.

Location Gallerie dell'Accademia (➤ 31)

Carpaccio's Two Women

St Ursula

Carpaccio's painting cycle in the Accademia tells the story of St Ursula, daughter of the Breton King Maurus, and her proposed marriage to Hereus, son of the English King Conon. It was agreed that the ceremony would take place on two conditions: first, that Hereus wait three years, and second that he convert to Christianity and accompany Ursula on a pilgrimage to Rome. Neither demand seemed unreasonable, except that the pilgrimage was to be made in the company of '11,000 virgins', and that the whole party would be massacred at Cologne on their return from Rome.

Carpaccio's St George Slaying the Dragon

CHURCHES

See also listings in the Top 25 Sights (► 24–48)

I GESUITI

This large, dank church, built by the Jesuits in 1715, is renowned for its extraordinary marble *trompe-l'œil*, best seen in the pulpit on the left, whose solid stone is carved to resemble pelmets, tassels and curtains. The church also boasts Titian's *Martyrdom of St Lawrence* (first chapel on the left) and Tintoretto's *Assumption of the Virgin* (left transept).

✚ G10–H10 ☒ Campo dei Gesuiti ☎ 041 528 6579 ☻ Daily 10–noon, 5–7 ⛴ Fondamente Nuove 52 ♿ Good 🆓 Free

SAN FRANCESCO DELLA VIGNA

San Francesco takes its name from a vineyard (*vigna*) left to the Franciscans here in 1253. Many alterations have been made since, not least the façade, built by Palladio between 1562 and 1572. Despite its shabby surroundings, the church has many fine tombs, marble reliefs by Pietro Lombardo, a delightful cloister and several good paintings, the best being Antonio da Negroponte's *Madonna and Child* (1450), on the right-hand wall of the right transept.

✚ J11 ☒ Campo della Confraternità ☎ 041 520 6102 ☻ Daily 8–noon, 3:30–7 ⛴ San Zaccaria or Celestia 1, 52, 82 ♿ Good 🆓 Free

SAN GIACOMO DELL'ORIO

Few Venetian buildings feel as old as San Giacomo, founded in the 9th century and added to over the years to produce a pleasing architectural hybrid. The 14th-century Gothic ship's-keel ceiling is outstanding, as is the wooden Tuscan statue of the *Madonna and Child*. There are magnificent paintings in the old and new sacristies (some by Veronese), two ancient marble pillars in the nave (stolen during the Fourth Crusade), a *Crucifix* by Lorenzo Veneziano, and a high altarpiece by Lorenzo Lotto of the *Madonna and Child* (1546).

✚ E10 ☒ Campo San Giacomo dell'Orio ☎ 041 524 0672 ☻ Mon–Sat 10–5:30; Sun 3–5:30 ⛴ Riva di Biasio or San Stae 1 ♿ Good 🆓 Cheap

SAN GIOBBE

San Giobbe began life as a 13th-century chapel dedicated to Job (Giobbe), a figure invoked against the plague. The fine portal and its four saints (1471) are the work of Pietro Lombardo. The interior is known for the Cappella Martini, created for expatriate silk-weavers from Lucca – hence the majolica work by the

Gesuiti trompe-l'oeil

Archway

Not far from San Giacomo, *en route* for Santa Maria Gloriosa dei Frari, stands the Scuola Grande di San Giovanni Evangelista. Once among the city's richest *scuole*, it was responsible, among other things, for commissioning the great 'Miracles of the True Cross' cycle now in the Accademia (► 31). Today, its buildings are mostly given over to conferences and are closed to the public.

Anyone, however, can enjoy its stunning archway, designed by Pietro Lombardo in 1481. The eagle in the lunette is the symbol of St John (San Giovanni).

Campanile, San Francesco della Vigna

Tuscan della Robbia family. The lions in the right aisle decorate the tomb of a 17th-century French ambassador. The sacristy off the right nave has a lovely ceiling and a fine triptych by Antonio Vivarini.

✚ D9 ✉ Campo San Giobbe ☎ 041 524 1889 🕓 Daily 10–noon, 4–6 🚤 Ponte dei Tre Archi 52 ♿ Good 💲 Free

SANTA MARIA DEL GIGLIO

This church takes its alternative name (Santa Maria Zobenigo) from the Jubanico family, who reputedly financed its building in the 9th century. Another family, the 17th-century Barbaro clan, commissioned the present façade. Its five statues represent five of the Barbaro brothers, while the martial reliefs depict fortresses that featured in the brothers' military careers. Inside, the high altar is adorned with works by Tintoretto, although the church's highlight is its lovingly displayed collection of saints' relics.

✚ F13 ✉ Campo Santa Maria Zobenigo ☎ 041 522 5739 or 041 275 0462 🕓 Mon–Sat 10–5:30; Sun 3–5:30 🚤 Santa Maria del Giglio 1 ♿ Poor (steps inside church) 💲 Cheap

SAN NICOLÒ DEI MENDICOLI

San Nicolò is one of Venice's oldest and most charming churches. It was built in the 12th century, and since 1966 has been restored by the Venice in Peril Fund. The interior is beautifully decorated with marbles, statues, paintings and fine gilded woodwork.

✚ B12–C12 ✉ Campo San Nicolò ☎ 041 528 5952 🕓 Mon–Sat 10–noon, 4–5:30; Sun 4–6 🚤 San Basilio 82 ♿ Good 💲 Free

SAN PANTALON

San Pantalon is best known for its gargantuan ceiling painting, Gian Antonio Fumiani's *The Miracles and Martyrdom of St Pantaleone* (1704). Smaller paintings include Veronese's *St Pantaleone Healing a Boy* (1587; second chapel on the right) and the *Coronation of the Virgin* (1444) by Antonio Vivarini and Giovanni d'Alemagna (chapel to the left as you face the chancel).

✚ D12 ✉ Campo San Pantalon ☎ 041 523 5893 🕓 8–11:30; 3:30–7; Sat 4:30–7 🚤 San Tomà 1, 82 ♿ Good 💲 Free

SAN POLO

Founded in 837 but much altered since, the church of San Polo is renowned for Giandomenico Tiepolo's *Via Crucis*, or *Stations of the Cross* (1747), an 18-panel cycle of paintings in the sacristy. Tintoretto's turbulent *Last Supper* (1547) hangs to the sacristy's left (on the west wall), while the apse chapel to the left of the high altar contains Veronese's *Marriage of the Virgin*.

✚ E11–F11 ✉ Campo San Polo ☎ 041 523 7631 or 041 275 0462 🕓 Mon–Sat 10–5:30; Sun 3–5:30 ♿ Good 💲 Cheap

Minor churches

During your exploration of the city look out for the following:

● Gesuati – notable for its richly decorated interior, a ceiling fresco by G B Tiepolo and paintings by Tintoretto, Piazzetta and Sebastiano Ricci (✚ E13).

● San Giacomo di Rialto – a tiny 5th-century church, reputedly Venice's oldest, known for its Gothic portico and lovely clock (✚ G11).

● San Moisè – with the most elaborate baroque façade in the city; look out for the many grotesques (✚ G12).

● San Salvatore – with a beautiful Renaissance interior and two paintings by Titian: *The Annunciation* (third altar on the right) and *The Transfiguration* above the high altar (✚ G11).

● San Trovaso – containing Tintoretto's final two works (either side of the choir) and the superb *St Chrysogonus on Horseback* (chapel left of the high altar) by Michele Giambono (✚ E13).

San Nicolò dei Mendicoli

SQUARES

See Top 25 Sights for
PIAZZA SAN MARCO (➤ 36)

CAMPO DEI MORI

This sleepy little square may take its name either from the Moorish merchants who traded on the *fondaco* near by, or from three silk merchants – Robia, Sandi and Alfani Mastelli – who left the Peloponnese (Morea) in 1112 to settle in the Palazzo Mastelli north of the *campo* (recognisable by the bas-relief of a camel). In time they may have inspired the so-called *Mori* (Moors), three statues built into the walls of the piazza's houses. The building just east of the square at No. 3399 (with a plaque) was home to the painter Tintoretto between 1574 and his death in 1594.

➕ F9 ⊠ Cannaregio ▤ Madonna dell'Orto 52

CAMPO SANTI GIOVANNI E PAOLO

The church of Santi Giovanni e Paolo in this square should not distract you from the statue of Bartolomeo Colleoni at its centre, nor the lovely façade of the Scuola Grande di San Marco on its northern flank. The *scuola*, now a hospital, was once the wealthiest in Venice and boasted a headquarters that was rivalled only by the Scuola Grande di San Rocco (➤ 27). Its façade was begun in 1487 by Pietro Lombardo (responsible for many of the sculptures in the church) and completed eight years later by Mauro Coducci, an architect active in the nearby churches of Santa Maria Formosa and San Zaccaria (➤ 42 and 45). The statue of Colleoni (1481–96), often called Italy's greatest equestrian sculpture, is mostly the work of the Florentine sculptor Andrea Verrocchio. Colleoni was a famous *condottiere*, or mercenary soldier (see panel), who left his vast fortune to Venice on the condition that the city erected a statue of him in Piazza San Marco. The state took his money, but was unwilling to glorify any individual in its most famous square and so slyly erected a statue in the more modest *Campo* San Marco instead.

➕ H11 ⊠ Castello 🍴 Cafés ▤ Ospedale Civile 52

CAMPO SANTA MARGHERITA

This may well become your favourite Venetian square, thanks mainly to its friendly and informal air, its collection of pleasant little bars and cafés, and its easy-going streetlife, which reminds you that Venice is still – just – a living city. Venetians meet here to chat, shop and sip coffee while their children play raucously on the square's ancient flagstones. Causin, noted for its ice cream, is the longest

Bartolomeo Colleoni

Born in Bergamo, Colleoni began his military career in Naples aged 19, entering Venetian service in 1431. After spells working for Milan, he returned to the Venetian cause in 1455. Over the next 20 years, however, he was called upon to fight only once. His name is a corruption of *coglioni*, meaning 'testicles', a play on words of which Colleoni was proud (*coglioni* featured conspicuously on his emblem). Thomas Coryat, an English traveller to Venice in 1611, repeated a story (put about by Colleoni himself) that 'Bathelmew Coleon…had his name from having *three* stones, for the Italian word Coglione doth signifie a testicle.'

Piazza San Marco

established of the cafés, but Il Caffè
and Il Doge are both equally fine places
to sit and watch the world go by. The
square is well-placed for many sights,
notably San Pantalon (► 53), the Scuola
Grande dei Carmini (► 26), San
Sebastiano (► 25), the Scuola Grande di
San Rocco and Frari (► 27 and 28), the
Accademia (► 31) and the Ca'
Rezzonico (► 29)

🚩 D12 ⊠ Dorsoduro 🍴 Cafés 🚤 Ca'
Rezzonico 1

CAMPO SANTA MARIA FORMOSA

Like all of Venice's more intriguing
squares, Campo Santa Maria Formosa is
distinguished by an authentic
atmosphere, its charm assured by a
combination of market stalls, local
streetlife and a succession of welcoming
cafés and bars. Although only a stone's
throw from Piazza San Marco, the
square escapes the attention of most
tourists but is convenient for several
key sights, not least of which is the church of Santa
Maria Formosa, whose crumbling façade dominates
its southern flank (► 42).

🚩 H11 ⊠ Castello 🍴 Cafés 🚤 Rialto 1, 3, 82

CAMPO SAN POLO

Campo San Polo is the largest of Venice's squares
after Piazza San Marco, but sits at the heart of the
smallest of the city's six *sestieri*. Once the scene of
bullfights, mass sermons and masked balls, it is now a
homely setting for elderly matrons and their dogs,
and groups of mothers with their children, who play
football and ride their bikes. Informal cafés with
outside tables provide a vantage point to watch the
many comings and goings, while the church of San
Polo (► 53) and the Palazzo Soranzo (once home to
Casanova) add a touch of decorum to the proceedings.

🚩 E11–F11 ⊠ San Polo 🍴 Cafés 🚤 San Silvestro 1

CAMPO SANTO STEFANO (CAMPO FRANCESCO MOROSINI)

After Campo Santa Margherita, this is probably the
most pleasant square in which to take a break from
sightseeing, and in particular from the church of
Santo Stefano (► 30) and the nearby Accademia
(► 31). Until 1802 it was used for bullfights, during
which bulls or oxen were tied to a stake and baited by
dogs. For years the area was grassy, all except for a
stone avenue known as the Liston. This became such
a popular place to stroll that it led to a Venetian
expression *andare al liston*, meaning 'to go for a walk'.
The square's nicest café is Paolin, considered by
many to serve the best ice cream in the city.

🚩 F12 ⊠ San Marco 🍴 Cafés 🚤 San Samuele 3, 4, 82

Campo Santa Margherita

Sior Antonio

A fourth figure complements
Campo dei Mori's three famous
Moorish statues. Known as Sior
Antonio Rioba, and distinguished
by its rusty metal nose, it peers
down from the corner of a building
on the east of the square.
Anonymous denunciations of the
state were once signed with his
name and left pinned at his feet, a
practice recalling 'Pasqualino' in
Rome, a statue at which
pasquinades (usually papal
denunciations) were left.

VIEWS

View from the Campanile

People-watching

The Loggia dei Cavalli is home to the famous bronze horses of the Basilica di San Marco (though today's versions are copies), but it also offers a tremendous view over Piazza San Marco and its swirling crowds. There are few better places in the whole of Italy to indulge in people-watching. 🚏 G12–H12 ✉ Piazza San Marco ☎ 041 522 5205 🕐 Mon–Fri 9:30–5:30; Sun 1–5:30 🍴 Piazza San Marco 🚢 San Marco or San Zaccaria 1, 3, 4, 52, 82 🚹 Poor 💰 Cheap

CAMPANILE

You will probably need to queue for the Campanile, but the view – which extends to the Alps on a clear day – is more than worth the wait. Goethe first saw the sea from here, while Galileo used the panorama to demonstrate his telescope. 🚏 G12 ✉ Piazza San Marco ☎ 041 522 4064 🕐 Jul–Aug: 9:30–7:30. Rest of year: 9:30 to between 3:30 and 7 🍴 Piazza San Marco 🚢 San Marco or San Zaccaria 1, 3, 4, 52, 82 🚹 Poor 💰 Moderate

PONTE DELL'ACCADEMIA

All the bridges across the Grand Canal offer mesmerising views, but none are perhaps as pretty as those from the Ponte dell'Accademia. Below you boats and gondolas flit about, while the Grand Canal curves gently to the east and west, offering views of distant palaces and the church of Santa Maria della Salute (► 34). 🚏 E13 ✉ Canal Grande 🚢 Accademia 1, 3, 4, 82 🚹 Poor 💰 Free

PONTE DI RIALTO

While the Ponte dell'Accademia offers a sublime general view of the Grand Canal, the Ponte di Rialto provides an overview of a stretch that is narrow yet frantically busy. You could spend a lot of time here simply soaking in the comings and goings beneath you, or casting your eye over the people jostling for position on the Fondamenta del Vin. 🚏 G11 ✉ Canal Grande 🕐 Always open 🍴 Cafés on the Fondamenta del Vin 🚢 Rialto 1, 3, 82 🚹 Poor 💰 Free

PUNTA DELLA DOGANA

The *sestiere* of Dorsoduro narrows to a point at the Punta della Dogana to offer a fine view across the mouth of the Grand Canal to the north (taking in the Campanile and Palazzo Ducale) and across the Canale della Giudecca to the south (with excellent views of San Giorgio Maggiore and the Giudecca). 🚏 G13 ✉ Canal Grande 🕐 Always open 🚢 Santa Maria della Salute 1 🚹 Good 💰 Free

SAN GIORGIO MAGGIORE

The view from the bell tower of Palladio's church is perhaps the best in the city, surpassing that of the Campanile by virtue of the fact that it offers a panorama which *includes* the Campanile and offers a better overview of the lagoon and the Giudecca. 🚏 H14 ✉ Campo San Giorgio, Isola di San Giorgio Maggiore ☎ 041 528 9900 🕐 Mon–Sat 9:30–12:30, 2:30–5; Sun 9:30–10:30, 2:30–5. Check as times can vary (particularly in winter) 🍴 Giudecca 🚢 San Giorgio 82 🚹 Poor 💰 Cheap

FAÇADES

CA' PESARO

Like many of Venice's finest palaces, the Ca' Pesaro presents its best face to the Grand Canal, but with some judicious route-finding its waterfront façade can also be glimpsed from the ends of several alleys off the Strada Nova. It was bought as three separate buildings in 1628 by the Pesaro family, who subsequently commissioned Baldassare Longhena, one of Venice's leading 17th-century architects, to unite the component parts behind one of the city's grandest baroque façades. Today it houses Venice's Museo Orientale, a collection of Chinese and Japanese art and artefacts.

🔲 F10 ✉ Canal Grande-Fondamenta Pesaro ☎ Museo Orientale 041 524 1173 🏛 Museo Orientale Tue–Sun 9–2 🚤 San Stae 1 ♿ Poor 💰 Museo Orientale: moderate

PALAZZO DARIO

The Palazzo Dario possesses perhaps the most charming façade of any Venetian palace, its appeal heightened by the building's rather alarming lean. Built in the 1480s, it was probably designed by Pietro Lombardo, whose use of inlaid coloured marbles is repeated in his masterpiece, Santa Maria dei Miracoli (➤ 41). It has long been believed that the palace is cursed. It is best seen from the Grand Canal or the Santa Maria del Giglio landing stage opposite.

🔲 F13 ✉ Calle Barbaro 🏛 Not open to the public 🚤 Santa Maria del Giglio 1

PALAZZO VENDRAMIN-CALERGI

The masterpiece of the Grand Canal, this palace was begun by Mauro Coducci at the end of the 15th century and finished in the first decade of the 16th century, probably by Tullio Lombardo. The composer Richard Wagner occupied a 15-room suite here during his last months. When he died in the palace in February 1883, his body was taken to the station by gondola in the dead of night for subsequent burial at Bayreuth. Today, the palace is the winter home of the Casinò Municipale. The façade is best seen from the Canal or from the Calle del Megio opposite.

🔲 F10 ✉ Canal Grande-Calle Larga Vendramin 🚤 San Marcuola 1, 82

Façades

A palace's waterfront façade was the most elaborate and the only one faced with stone, which was both costlier and heavier than brick, and therefore a burden on the building's foundations (these consisted of wooden piles driven into the mud). The ground floor was marked by a gate opening onto the canal and entrance hall (*andron*), used for deliveries and access by gondola. Above, windows mark the *mezzanino*, a labyrinth of small rooms used as offices, and above them a row of larger windows which indicate the *piano nobile*, the grandest of the palace's living areas. This consisted of suites arranged around the *portego*, a broad corridor through the building that encouraged cool breezes to pass through in summer.

Façade of the Palazzo Dario

BOAT TRIPS

Vaporetto *on the Grand Canal*

Gondola rides

Hiring a gondola is an enchanting but expensive business. In theory, the official tariff is around L80,000 for a 50-minute ride for up to five passengers, rising to about L100,000 for the same trip between 8PM and 8AM. An extra L40,000 or so is levied for each additional 25 minutes, and more for any musical accompaniment. In practice, rates are more negotiable, so confirm the rate *and* the duration of a trip before departure. Do not be afraid to walk away or haggle if the prices seem too high – there are plenty of gondoliers. Most gondoliers have a set route, so if you wish to see a particular part of the city discuss this before fixing a price. Also note the location of various official stands: Riva del Carbon (near the Rialto); Campo San Moisè; Santa Maria del Giglio; Bacino Orseolo (north-west of Piazza San Marco); at the railway station; and the Danieli hotel.

See Top 25 Sights for
CANAL GRANDE (► 24)

ISLANDS
The No. 12 steamer from the Fondamente Nuove runs every 60 to 90 minutes to the islands of Burano and Torcello, a 45-minute trip that offers not only two interesting end destinations, but also provides excellent views of Venice and the Venetian lagoon. (See panel ► 21 for details of the *Biglietto Isole*, a special 'Islands Ticket'.)

🚩 H10 ✉ Fondamente Nuove 🚤 Fondamente Nuove 12 💷 Expensive

LA GIUDECCA AND THE DOCKS
Catching *vaporetto* 82 at San Zaccaria and staying on board past San Giorgio and the Giudecca to Piazzale Roma will give you not only a good view of San Giorgio Maggiore and the Giudecca ahead (and San Marco behind), but also an interesting insight into the area around the docks and Stazione Marittima, the busy and little-visited commercial port area in the south-east of the city.

🚩 H12 ✉ Riva degli Schiavoni 🚤 San Zaccaria 82 💷 Moderate

LIDO
In the late 19th century the Lido – which lies 20 minutes south of Venice by boat – was one of the most exclusive bathing establishments in Europe. This is less true today and, unless you wish to spend time on a beach during your stay, the island is best seen from the No. 1 *vaporetto*, which can be boarded at any of the stops on the Grand Canal or San Zaccaria. The service provides fine views back to San Marco and a glimpse at enough of the Lido to satisfy most people's curiosity.

🚩 H12 ✉ Riva degli Schiavoni 🚤 San Zaccaria 1 💷 Moderate

MURANO AND ARSENALE
The Arsenale, Venice's vast former shipyards, are now occupied by the military and are out of bounds to the general public. The only way to catch a glimpse of the yards, whose boats provided the wherewithal for Venice's supremacy at sea, is to take the No. 521 boat from Tana. This is permitted to pass through a canal that bisects the yards, and has the added advantage that it continues to Murano, circles the island, and then returns to the Fondamente Nuove before proceeding around the northern shore of the city to the Canale di Cannaregio and Piazzale Roma.

🚩 K12–K13 ✉ Campiello della Malvasia 🚤 Tana 521 💷 Moderate

FREE ATTRACTIONS

See Top 25 Sights for
BASILICA DI SAN MARCO (► 39)
CANAL GRANDE (► 24)
SAN GIOVANNI IN BRAGORA (► 47)
SANTI GIOVANNI E PAOLO (► 43)
SANTA MARIA DEI MIRACOLI (► 41)

CHURCHES

Churches rarely charge, and where they do, as in the case of the Frari (► 28), the entrance fee is invariably modest. Most have some artistic treasure – a sculpture, a Tintoretto, a Bellini altarpiece – which makes a visit more than worthwhile (► 50–51 and 52–53).

THE CITY

Venice's finest free sight is Venice itself, for no city in the world offers as many beautiful views, intriguing streets and magical buildings. Almost any walk has its rewards, the more so if you stroll around the city early in the morning or late at night (► 16–18 and 56).

MUSIC

You may occasionally come across free organ, choral or chamber recitals in Venetian churches. Look out for posters or contact the tourist office for details. Mass is usually sung in the Basilica di San Marco at 9AM on weekdays and 10AM on Sundays and feast days. Vespers are sung at 5:30PM in winter and 6PM in summer.

PAINTINGS

Many of Venice's finest paintings are visible for free. These include masterpieces by Veronese (► 25), Tintoretto (► 33), Titian (► 52), and the Bellini altarpieces of San Pietro Martire, Santi Giovanni e Paolo and San Zaccaria (► 20, 43 and 45).

RIALTO MARKETS

The Rialto has it all, whether you want to shop for souvenirs, people-watch or revel in the sights and smells of the area's famous markets. Early in the morning, before the crowds arrive, is the best time for a stroll around the fantastic medley of food and fish stalls (► 81).

SQUARES

Venetian squares offer the chance not only to watch your fellow visitors, but also provide an opportunity to take in the Venetians at work and play. Most squares have a variety of cafés with outside tables. For the price of a cup of coffee you can observe everything from the comfort of a café terrace (► 54–55).

Parks and gardens

Venice is a city whose peculiar make-up means it has little room left over for public parks and gardens. This said, there are one or two areas of green space. In the heart of the city these are restricted to the small Giardinetti Reali (█ G12–G13) immediately south of Piazza San Marco (but entered from the waterfront). On the city's fringes are the much larger Giardini Pubblici (█ L14) and more modest Giardino Papadopoli (█ C11–D11). Further afield, the islands of Burano and Torcello have extensive areas of open space (► 20–21).

Giardini Pubblici

ATTRACTIONS FOR CHILDREN

Restaurants

Pizzerias and more down-market restaurants usually welcome children, though special facilities such as high chairs are rarely available. If you want a small serving ask for *una mezza porzione*. Smarter restaurants on the whole do not take kindly to smaller children, though the Italians are generally far more tolerant of children in public places than many northern Europeans.

Carnival masks

BOAT TRIPS

Children should be captivated by the things to see from Venice's *vaporetti* and *motoscafi*. The best short trip is along the Grand Canal (► 24), while the best longer journey (on a larger boat) is out to the islands of Burano, Murano and Torcello (► 20–21).

GLASS-BLOWING

Many of the glass workshops and showrooms on Murano (► 20) offer the chance to watch glass-blowers in action, a novelty that should appeal to children (glass-blowers can also usually be encouraged to make a small glass gift for children to take away). Enquire at the tourist office for details of factories currently open to the public.

GONDOLAS

Gondolas are large enough to accommodate at least two adults and two children, and are rented by time rather than the number of passengers, so taking children should not add to the cost. See panel ► 58 for details of prices and how to hire gondolas. Note that Grand Canal rides can be choppy.

ICE CREAM

Italian ice cream should satisfy the most demanding of young palates. Some of Venice's best *gelato* is to be found at Paolin in Campo Santo Stefano (Campo Francesco Morosini), Causin in Campo Santa Margherita and Nico on the Zattere ai Gesuati (► 74–75 for more details).

LIDO

The Lido offers the chance for children to swim or play on the beach, as well as the excitement of the boat trip from Venice (take *vaporetto* No. 1). It is also possible to rent bikes and pedalos at several outlets along the promenade. Note that many of the Lido's beaches are owned by hotels; public beaches (*spiaggia* or *zona comunale*) are clearly marked.

MARKETS

The strange sights, sounds and smells of the Rialto markets (► 81) should appeal to children of all ages, although the more bizarre and bloody seafood of the Pescheria (fish market) may upset younger children.

MASKS

Children might enjoy buying and wearing Venice's famous masks, or simply window shopping among some of the city's better known mask shops (► 78–79). It can also be fun to watch masks being made at some of the larger workshops.

VENICE
where to...

LUXURY HOTELS

Prices

Expect to pay for a double room per night:

Luxury   over L500,000

Expensive   L250–500,000

Mid-range   L150–300,000

Budget   under L170,000

Italy's hotels, including those in Venice, are classified by the state into five categories, from one star (basic) to five stars (luxury). The prices of individual rooms should be displayed in the lobby and in the room itself. Prices for different rooms often vary within a hotel, so if a room is too expensive be sure to ask if another one is available for less (you may well be shown the most expensive room first). Watch out for supplements for breakfast, which may be charged even if you do not take it, and in peak periods remember that hotels may insist that you take half- or full board.

CIPRIANI ****

Venice's most expensive hotel is a relative newcomer to Venice, having opened in 1963, but has quickly become a byword for luxury. Facilities include a Jacuzzi in every suite, an Olympic-sized swimming-pool, butler service and a renowned restaurant. The location in gardens on the eastern end of the Giudecca is away from the tourist hustle, but can make you feel slightly isolated from the city. Most rooms have superb views.

✚ H14 ⊠ Giudecca 10 ☎ 041 520 7744; fax 041 520 3930 ⛴ Zitelle 52, 82 ⚓ Private launch service

DANIELI *****

A hotel since 1822, the Danieli ranks as one of the finest of Venice's luxury hotels, and is the choice of visiting royalty, politicians and other VIPs. You should endeavour to make sure your room is in the old wing of the Gothic *palazzo* rather than the newer controversial annexe built in 1948.

✚ H12 ⊠ Riva degli Schiavoni-Calle delle Rasse, Castello 4196 ☎ 041 522 6480; fax 041 520 0208 ⛴ San Zaccaria 1, 4, 52, 82

EUROPA E REGINA *****

Venice's 'Big Three' – the Gritti, Cipriani and Danieli – tend to overshadow this CIGA-owned hotel, but its prices are some of the most reasonable, relatively speaking, of the city's luxury hotels. Most of its 192 rooms are spacious and many enjoy glorious views over a courtyard garden or across the Grand Canal, while the restaurant's canal terrace and garden are wonderfully evocative places to dine.

✚ G13 ⊠ Calle Larga (Viale) XXII Marzo, San Marco 2159 ☎ 041 520 0477; fax 041 523 1533 ⛴ San Marco or Santa Maria del Giglio 1, 3, 4, 82

GRITTI PALACE *****

Not the most expensive hotel in Venice, but – along with the Danieli – the one traditionally considered to have the most class and *élan*. Greta Garbo, Winston Churchill and a host of other VIPs are among its past guests. Housed in a 15th-century *palazzo* close to the Grand Canal, its 93 rooms, reception areas and service are all impeccably grand. Private launch and private beach available.

✚ F13 ⊠ Santa Maria del Giglio, San Marco 2467 ☎ 041 794611; fax 041 520 0942 ⛴ Santa Maria del Giglio 1

MONACO AND GRAND CANAL ****

Not as famous as other hotels in its class, but almost equally stylish and elegant. As its name suggests, it overlooks the Grand Canal near the Punta della Dogana, and the nicest of its 71 rooms enjoys views across to Santa Maria della Salute. Excellent restaurant and magnificent terrace.

✚ G13 ⊠ Calle Vallaresso, San Marco 1325 ☎ 041 520 0211; fax 041 520 0501 ⛴ San Marco 1, 3, 4, 82

EXPENSIVE HOTELS

ACCADEMIA-VILLA MARAVEGE ★★★
A 17th-century *palazzo* located just west of the Accademia that once housed the Russian Embassy. Its popular 27 rooms are still grand and are furnished with antiques, although some are rather small. There is also a garden with a Grand Canal view.
✚ E13 ✉ Fondamenta Bollani, Dorsoduro 1058 ☎ 041 521 0188; fax 041 523 9152 ⛴ Accademia 1, 3, 4, 82

CAVALLETTO E DOGE ★★★★
This 95-room hotel north of Piazza San Marco has been in business for over 200 years. Good restaurant; light and airy rooms.
✚ G12 ✉ Calle Cavalletto, San Marco 1107 ☎ 041 520 0955; fax 041 523 8184 ⛴ San Marco 1, 3, 4, 82

GIORGIONE ★★★★
This 69-room hotel has modern facilities and is one of the best in the category. Rooms decorated in period style, with elegant fabrics and fine attention to detail.
✚ G10 ✉ Campo Santi Apostoli, Cannaregio 4587 ☎ 041 522 5810; fax 041 523 9092 ⛴ Ca' d'Oro 1

METROPOLE ★★★★
An elegant and sophisticated hotel with 74 rooms on the busy waterfront by the church of the Pietà. Rooms are spacious and romantic, decorated with antiques, paintings and period furniture. Some rooms have broad lagoon views.
J12 ✉ Riva degli Schiavoni 4149 ☎ 041 520 5044; fax 041 522 3679 ⛴ San Marco 1, 3, 4, 82

SAN MOISÈ ★★★
The 16 rooms in this tranquil but centrally located hotel – formerly a medieval grain store – vary in size, but all are furnished with Murano glass lamps, old mirrors and other antique touches.
✚ F12 ✉ Piscina San Moisè, San Marco 2058 ☎ 041 520 3755; fax 041 521 0670 ⛴ San Marco or Santa Maria del Giglio 1, 3, 4, 82

SATURNIA & INTERNAZIONALE ★★★★
Romantic, old-fashioned hotel in a peacefull setting. All 95 rooms differ slightly in style; the best look on to the courtyard garden.
✚ F12–13 ✉ Calle Larga (Viale) XXII Marzo, San Marco 2398 ☎ 041 520 8377; fax 041 520 7131 ⛴ Santa Maria del Giglio 1

SCANDINAVIA ★★★
There is considerable variety in the 27 rooms of this fine hotel, but all are comfortable and spacious. Good location on one of Venice's nicest squares.
✚ H11 ✉ Campo Santa Maria Formosa, Castello 5240 ☎ 041 522 3507; fax 041 523 5232 ⛴ Rialto 1, 3, 82

STURION ★★★
The best of this welcoming hotel's 11 rooms – which vary in price – look over the Grand Canal. Some non-smoking rooms.
✚ F11 ✉ Calle del Storione, San Polo 679 ☎ 041 523 6243; fax 041 522 8378 ⛴ San Silvestro 1

Hotels

Venice has been accommodating visitors for hundreds of years, although over the last couple of decades the sheer number of tourists to the city has strained its 200 or so hotels to capacity, and brought about a slide in standards among the more cynical hoteliers (who know they are guaranteed customers however grim their properties). Prices are also higher than in most of Italy (see panel opposite), and booking is now a virtual necessity all year round (see panel ➤ 64). Noise, location and actually finding a room are other important considerations (see panels ➤ 65–67).

63

MID-RANGE HOTELS

Booking

It is now almost essential to reserve a room in Venice for July and August, and wise to do so during the rest of the high season. Officially the high season runs from 15 March to 15 November and from 21 December to 6 January, but it now effectively includes the period of *Carnevale* in February. Many hotels do not recognise a low season, however, and lower category hotels where you might have been able to negotiate cheaper off-season rates often close during the winter. Some hotels accept credit-card reservations over the phone, but it is always best (having phoned or faxed first) to send a firm deposit in the shape of a Eurocheque (made out in lire) or International Money Order. Follow this up with a confirmation of receipt and another call or fax a few days before departure to confirm your booking.

AGLI ALBORETTI **

This 20-room hotel was added to the fine restaurant downstairs in 1982. Attractively located on a tree-lined street and convenient to the Accademia and Zattere. Rooms are modern and smart, if a little small, and there is a pleasant garden. Extremely popular, especially with UK and US visitors.

✚ E13 ◻ Rio Terrà Sant'Agnese-Antonio Foscarini, Dorsoduro 884 ☎ 041 523 0058; fax 041 521 0158 ◻ Accademia or Zattere 1, 3, 4, 52, 82

AMERICAN ***

A 29-room hotel just two minutes' walk from the Accademia, but on a small canal away from the crowds. Rooms range in price and quality but most have lots of wood and period touches. Lovely terrace and vine-shaded breakfast area.

✚ E13 ◻ Fondamenta Bragadin, Rio di San Vio, Dorsoduro 628 ☎ 041 520 4733; fax 041 520 4048 ◻ Accademia 1, 3, 4, 82

BOSTON ***

On one of Venice's main shopping streets within easy reach of Piazza San Marco. The 42 rooms vary in terms of furnishings and views; most are smallish, but comfortable and well-designed.

✚ G12 ◻ Calle dei Fabbri, San Marco 848 ☎ 041 528 7665; fax 041 522 6628 ◻ Rialto or San Marco 1, 3, 4, 82

CASANOVA ***

This comfortable hotel has 44 rooms and is in the heart of the shopping district close to Piazza San Marco. Fittings in rooms are mostly modern; public spaces have fine old furniture and antique mirrors.

✚ G12 ◻ Frezzeria, San Marco 1284 ☎ 041 520 6855; fax 041 520 6413 ◻ San Marco 1, 3, 4, 82

CLUB CRISTAL

A pleasant bed-and-breakfast of three-star standard in a quiet street near the Campo dei Gesuiti, with a pretty roof terrace for evening meals on request. English owners. Five spacious rooms, plus annexe accommodation.

✚ G10 ◻ Calle Zanardi, Cannaregio 4133 ☎ 041 523 7194; fax 041 521 2705 ◻ Ca' d'Oro 1

DO POZZI ***

This quiet hotel has 29 rooms and is located in a pleasant courtyard square off Calle Larga (Viale) XXII Marzo close to Piazza San Marco. A mixture of modern and antique decor. Some rooms a touch cramped.

✚ F13–G13 ◻ Corte dei Due Pozzi, San Marco 2373 ☎ 041 520 7855; fax 041 522 9413 ◻ Santa Maria del Giglio or San Marco 1, 3, 4, 82

FALIER **

A small, well-presented hotel in a part of town that is less busy, but still convenient to Santa Maria Gloriosa dei Frari and the Scuola Grande di San Rocco. Some of the 19 rooms (13 with private bathroom) are a little small, but all are elegant and tidy, and prices are very reasonable.

🔲 D11 ✉ Salizzada San Pantalon, Santa Croce 130 ☎ 041 710882; fax 041 520 6554 🚤 Ferrovia or San Tomà 1, 3, 4, 52, 82

FLORA *

This 44-room hotel has gained a well-deserved reputation, thanks to its pleasant garden, though some rooms are rather small. Just off Calle Larga (Viale) XXII Marzo west of Piazza San Marco.

🔲 F13 ✉ Calle Bergamaschi, San Marco 2283/a ☎ 041 520 5844; fax 041 522 8217 🚤 Santa Maria del Giglio 1

KETTE *

Quiet location south-east of La Fenice opera house and well-placed for Piazza San Marco. Some of the 56 rooms are small for the price, but off-season the rates can be reasonable.

🔲 F12 ✉ Piscina San Moisè, San Marco 2053 ☎ 041 520 7766; fax 041 522 8964 🚤 San Marco or Santa Maria del Giglio 1, 3, 4, 82

LA CALCINA *

The waterfront location of this 35-room hotel and the nearby Pensione Seguso (see opposite) may not be to all tastes, but you are in an interesting area of the city well away from the bustle of central Venice. This is where the Victorian artist and writer John Ruskin spent much of his Venetian sojourn.

🔲 E13–E14 ✉ Fondamenta Zàttere ai Gesuati, Dorsoduro 780 ☎ 041 520 6466; fax 041 522 7045 🚤 Zàttere 52, 82

LA FENICE ET DES ARTISTES *

Pleasant hotel (once the home of painter Lorenzo Lotto). The 65 rooms are divided between linked buildings: modern and bland in one, elegant but faded in the other.

🔲 F12 ✉ Campiello Fenice, San Marco 1936 ☎ 041 523 2333; fax 041 520 3721 🚤 Santa Maria del Giglio 1

PENSIONE SEGUSO **

Favourable choice of hotel since almost all of its 36 traditionally furnished rooms have views across either the Giudecca or San Vio canals.

🔲 E13–E14 ✉ Fondamenta Zàttere ai Gesuati, Dorsoduro 779 ☎ 041 528 6858; fax 041 522 2340 🚤 Zàttere 52, 82

SAN CASSIANO-CA' FAVRETTO *

A lovely hotel full of atmosphere, occupying a converted 14th-century *palazzo* on the Grand Canal. Half the rooms face the Grand Canal, the rest look on to a side canal.

🔲 F10 ✉ Calle della Rosa, Santa Croce 2232 ☎ 041 524 1768; fax 041 721033 🚤 San Stae 1

SANTA MARINA *

Opened in 1990, this comfortable 16-room hotel is one of Venice's newest (the annexe is even newer). Off the tourist trail, but still extremely convenient for shopping and all the major sights. Bright rooms decorated in Venetian period style.

🔲 H11 ✉ Campo di Santa Marina, Castello 6068 ☎ 041 523 9202; fax 041 520 0907 🚤 Rialto 1, 3, 82

Noise

Although Venice is a remarkably quiet city, it still has its fair share of nocturnal traffic – even without cars. Church bells clang through the night, and pedestrian chatter in the main alleys and streets can reverberate noisily. Traffic on the main canals can also be surprisingly noisy, and refuse boats, *vaporetti* and food suppliers start up very early. This can put a different complexion on that apparently desirable room overlooking the Grand Canal.

BUDGET HOTELS

Location

Venice's best hotels line the Grand Canal near San Marco; the cheapest lie in the slightly grubby streets around the station and Lista di Spagna. Other concentrations of hotels are near the Rialto and in Dorsoduro, the latter being one of the city's less touristy locations. You will find the odd hotel in quiet backstreets, but there is no such thing as the 'undiscovered gem' in Venice. In a city as compact as Venice, however, even 'poor' hotels are rarely far from the sights. Be certain when booking a hotel to find its exact location – street name as well as number – and remember that you may well need to carry your luggage some distance.

AI DO MORI *

A friendly 11-room hotel (with just three bathrooms) in a busy location close to San Marco. The best rooms on the upper floor are small but have views over the Basilica di San Marco and the Torre dell' Orologio. Lower floor rooms are larger with modern and simple decor.

✚ G12–H12 ✉ Calle Larga San Marco, San Marco 658 ☎ 041 520 4817 or 041 528 9293; fax 041 520 5328 ⛴ San Marco or San Zaccaria 1, 3, 4, 52, 82

ALEX *

This hotel's excellent location near Santa Maria Gloriosa dei Frari and the Scuola Grande di San Rocco makes up for the slightly tired decor of the rooms.

✚ E11 ✉ Rio Terrà Frari, San Polo 2606 ☎ 041 523 1341; fax 041 523 1341 ⛴ San Tomà 1, 82

ANTICO CAPON *

Seven simple rooms above a good pizzeria-restaurant (► 72) on one of Venice's most informal squares. Amiable owners. Good location for sightseeing.

✚ D12 ✉ Campo Santa Margherita, Dorsoduro 3004/b ☎ 041 528 5292; fax 041 528 5292 ⛴ San Tomà or Ca' Rezzonico 1, 82

CA' FOSCARI *

This relaxed and well-appointed hotel offers ten rooms (none with private bathroom) and is hidden away in a little alley just south of San Tomà and Santa Maria Gloriosa dei Frari.

✚ E12 ✉ Calle della Frescada, Dorsoduro 3888 ☎ 041 910817 or 041 710401; fax 041 710817 ⛴ San Tomà or Ca' Rezzonico 1, 82

CANADA **

This immaculate 25-room hotel has several singles. The best room (a double) has its own roof terrace, but you need to book it well in advance. In the heart of the city between the Rialto and Campo Santa Maria Formosa.

✚ G11 ✉ Campo San Lio, Castello 5659 ☎ 041 522 9912; fax 041 523 5852 ⛴ Rialto 1, 3, 82

DA BRUNO **

An excellent location close to the Rialto outweighs the small size of the hotel's 32 rooms.

✚ G11–H11 ✉ Salizzada San Lio, Castello 5726/a ☎ 041 523 0452; fax 041 522 1157 ⛴ Rialto 1, 3, 82

PANTALON ***

Just east of San Pantalon on a bustling little shopping street, this 15-room hotel has recently been renovated, pushing up its once bargain prices to the top of the budget range. Near many places of interest and the attractive squares of Campo San Polo and Campo Santa Margherita.

✚ D12 ✉ Crosera San Pantalon, Dorsoduro 3942 ☎ 041 522 3646; fax 041 718683 ⛴ San Tomà 1, 82

DONI *

Intimate hotel in an attractive location

between the Basilica and San Zaccaria, away from busy Piazza San Marco. It has 13 clean, simple rooms (none with private bathroom), the best of which overlook the Riva del Vin or small garden

🏠 H12 ✉ Fondamenta del Vin, off Salizzada San Provolo, Castello 4656 ☎ 041 522 4267; fax 041 522 4267 🚤 San Zaccaria 1, 3, 4, 52, 82

FIORITA *

Very pretty, friendly and popular hotel in a quaint square (used for breakfast in summer) immediately north of Santo Stefano. Ten rooms with wood beamed ceilings and plain furnishings.

🏠 F12 ✉ Campiello Nuovo, San Marco 3457/a ☎ 041 523 4754; fax 041 522 8043 🚤 Accademia or Sant'Angelo 1, 3, 4, 82

MESSNER **

Located in a quiet corner of Dorsoduro, this hotel is very handy for the church of Santa Maria della Salute and Collezione Peggy Guggenheim. It has a lovely garden and 35 large, modern and recently renovated rooms. Try to stay in the main hotel rather than the nearby annexe or *dipendenza*.

🏠 F13 ✉ Rio Terrà del Spezier, Dorsoduro 216 ☎ 041 522 7443; fax 041 522 7266 🚤 Santa Maria della Salute 1

MONTIN *

Much of this hotel's fame derives from the well-known and expensive restaurant of the same name downstairs, although the ten rooms are

perfectly pleasant and larger and more comfortable than its one-star classification suggests.

🏠 D13 ✉ Fondamenta di Borgo, Dorsoduro 1147 ☎ 041 522 7151; fax 041 520 0255 🚤 Ca' Rezzonico or Accademia 1, 3, 4, 82

REMEDIO *

This 12-room hotel is on a tranquil side-street, in an excellent and peaceful central setting just 100m from Piazza San Marco. The furniture is simple and the views unexceptional, but the hotel is clean and the staff welcoming. The cheapest rooms share bathrooms.

🏠 H12 ✉ Calle del Rimedio, Castello 4412 ☎ 041 520 6232; fax 041 521 0485 🚤 San Marco 1, 3, 4, 82

SAN SAMUELE *

Some of the ten rooms here are pretty basic, but the general quality is much better than in many in this price range. Excellently located just north of Santo Stefano, with a welcoming owner.

🏠 E12 ✉ Salizzada San Samuele, San Marco 3358 ☎ 041 522 8045; fax 041 522 8045 🚤 Sant'Angelo 1

SILVA *

Friendly 25-room hotel (with nine bathrooms) just north of Piazza San Marco between San Zaccaria and Santa Maria Formosa on one of Venice's most attractive waterways.

🏠 H12 ✉ Fondamenta del Rimedio, Castello 4423 ☎ 041 522 7643 or 041 523 7892; fax 041 528 6817 🚤 San Zaccaria 1, 3, 4, 52, 82

Finding a room

By far the best thing to do is to plan ahead and book a room in advance (see panel ➤ 64). If you arrive in Venice without accommodation do not accept rooms from touts at the station unless you are desperate: most work for hotels near by. If you are tempted, ignore their inevitably warm reassurances and find out exactly where the hotel is located, how much the room will cost, whether it has a private bathroom and whether the cost of breakfast is additional. Otherwise, join the queues for rooms at the tourist offices at the train station, Tronchetto, the Autorimessa car park in Piazzale Roma, at Marco Polo Airport, or at the Mestre-Marghera exit of the A4 motorway. In desperation, you could take a train to Padua (30 minutes). Unless you are unable to find a room in the right price bracket, do not stay in Mestre, the ugly and largely industrial town on the mainland.

67

EXPENSIVE RESTAURANTS

Restaurants on the following pages are in three price categories:

Expensive   over L100,000
Mid-range   L65–100,000
Budget   under L65,000

Harry's Bar

This famous bar and restaurant was founded in 1931 when, according to legend, a now-forgotten American ('Harry') remarked to hotel barman Giuseppe Cipriani that Venice lacked for nothing except a good bar. The enterprising Cipriani duly sought financial backing, found an old rope store near Piazza San Marco, and Harry's Bar was born. It is now a place of high prices, good food and great cocktails, and – in the words of writer Gore Vidal – 'a babble of barbaric voices…the only place for Americans in acute distress to go for comfort and advice…'

AL COVO

Charming two-roomed restaurant in a calm, romantic and tasteful setting. It is usually possible to eat out in the adjacent little square in summer. The service is generally warm and polite – the owner's wife at front of house is American – while highly accomplished cooking focuses on Venetian recipes using the best ingredients. Fish dishes predominate the regularly changing menu (when there is one), servings are small, the cooking fresh and refined, and the wine list is good. Good-value set lunch. A fine alternative to the more bustling Corte Sconta nearby (➤ 70). With only 50 seats, be sure to book.

✚ J12 ✉ Campiello della Pescaria, Castello 3968 ☎ 041 522 3812 ⏰ Closed Wed, Thu and two weeks in Aug and Jan ⛴ Arsenale 1

ANTICA MONTIN

This venerable restaurant has been famous for several decades and is popular with the rich and famous, although today it depends somewhat on its former reputation. The quality of food is once again touching former heights; an evocative place to eat, either in the painting-lined dining room or on the shaded outside terrace.

✚ D13 ✉ Fondamenta di Borgo, Dorsoduro 1147 ☎ 041 522 7151 ⏰ Closed Tue evening, Wed ⛴ Zàttere or Ca' Rezzonico 1, 52, 82

ANTICO MARTINI

The Martini, established in the 18th century, has long been one of the city's most stylish restaurants. Classic Venetian cuisine fills the menu, with seafood playing a key role. The smart terrace overlooks La Fenice opera house and the wine list boasts 300 labels. Meals are served until 1AM.

✚ F12 ✉ Campo San Fantin, San Marco 1983 ☎ 041 522 4121 ⏰ Closed Tue, Wed lunch; dinner only Dec–mid-Mar ⛴ Santa Maria del Giglio 1

DA FIORE

This small highly acclaimed restaurant produces excellent Venetian cuisine, cooked by self-taught owners. Since appearing as one of the 'world's best' restaurants in an American publication, it has also become extremely difficult to get a table. Difficult to find.

✚ E11 ✉ Calle del Scaleter, San Polo 2002/a ☎ 041 721308 ⏰ Closed Sun, Mon ⛴ San Stae or San Silvestro 1

DANIELI TERRACE

Venice's smart hotels all have fine restaurants and the Danieli is no exception. Refined Venetian and international cooking is served with style and panache on the stylish outside terrace overlooking the Grand Canal. Fine service and excellent wine list, all at high prices.

✚ H12 ✉ Riva degli Schiavoni-Calle delle Rasse, Castello 4196 ☎ 041 522 6480 ⛴ San Zaccaria 1, 4, 52, 82

DO FORNI

This slightly self-conscious restaurant is known as one of *the* places to eat among locals and tourists alike. One dining room is furnished rustically and the other fashioned like an opulent *Orient Express* cabin. The number of tables and the menu have grown with the restaurant's success, but despite the chaos the food remains good – although at inflated prices.

✚ G12 ✉ Calle dei Specchieri, San Marco 468 ☎ 041 523 7729 🚊 San Marco 1, 3, 4, 82

HARRY'S BAR

This legendary establishment is best known for its celebrity status. The restaurant upstairs serves reliable fare (although it can be very good, many say it is not what it used to be), while snacks can be ordered at the downstairs bar. This is also a great place to come for cocktails – the Bellini was invented here.

✚ G13 ✉ Calle Vallaresso, San Marco 1323 ☎ 041 528 5777 🚊 San Marco 1, 3, 4, 82

HARRY'S DOLCI

What began as a glorified cake- and coffee-shop offshoot of Harry's Bar (see above) has turned into a restaurant every bit as good (and almost as expensive). The food is refined Venetian, while the atmosphere is smart without being at all intimidating.

✚ D14 ✉ Fondamenta San Biagio, Giudecca 773 ☎ 041 522 4844 🕔 Apr–Oct: daily

10:30–3PM, 7:30–10:30PM. Nov–Mar: closed Tue 🚊 Sant'Eufemia 52, 82

LA CARAVELLA

The interior of this restaurant, one of two in the Saturnia hotel (➤ 63), is decked out in the manner of a Venetian galley. The over-the-top decor fails to detract from the normally outstanding food, but it can be prone to lapses. The cooking has international as well as Venetian touches.

✚ F13 ✉ Calle Larga (Viale) XXII Marzo, San Marco 2398 ☎ 041 520 8901 🕔 Closed Wed in winter 🚊 Santa Maria del Giglio

LOCANDA CIPRIANI

The top-quality food served in a wonderful setting – facing the island's two churches – makes up for the hefty prices and pretentious decor.

✚ Off map ✉ Fondamenta dei Borgononi-Piazza Santa Fosca 29, Torcello ☎ 041 730150 🕔 Closed Tue in winter and Jan 🚊 Torcello 12, 14

POSTE VECIE

Ingredients could hardly be fresher than at this noted and appealing fish restaurant, in an old post-house alongside the Rialto's Pescheria fish market. The cooking is refined, but can be variable, and there's a good wine list. One of the oldest restaurants in Venice, reputedly founded in 1500.

✚ F10–F11 ✉ Campo della Pescaria, San Polo 1608 ☎ 041 721822 🕔 Closed Tue and four weeks in Jul and Aug 🚊 Rialto 1, 3, 82

Wines

Most of Venice's wine comes from the Veneto region on the mainland. Its best-known wines are the usually unexceptional Soave (white), and Valpolicella and Bardolino (reds). More interesting whites include Soave Classico, Bianco di Custoza, Tocai, Pinot Grigio and the wines of the Breganze region. The best white of all is Prosecco, a delicious dry sparkling wine often drunk as an aperitif. Interesting reds include Raboso, the wines of the Colle Berici and Lison-Pramaggiore regions, and two excellent dessert wines: Amarone and Recioto della Valpolicella.

Mid-Range Restaurants

Starters

Venice's best-known starters are *sarde in saôr* (sardines in a cold onion and vinegar marinade) or a simple mixed plate of seafood (*antipasto di mare*). *Prosciutto San Daniele* is the region's best ham. Pasta is available, usually with seafood – try *spaghetti alle vongole* (pasta with clams) – but most locals prefer rice, notably *risi e bisi* (rice, peas and ham) or risotto with seafood (*risotto di mare* or *dei pescatori*), mushrooms (*funghi*), vegetables, chicken and ham (*alla sbirraglia*), or flavoured with cuttlefish ink (*risotto in nero*). Tripe, snails and quail may also feature. Fish soup (*brodetto* or *zuppa di mare*) is another popular starter, as is pasta and bean soup (*pasta e fasioli*).

AGLI ALBORETTI

Convenient to the Accademia, just two minutes' walk away, this restaurant takes its name from the trees (*alberi*) outside. It is pretty inside and out, and in summer you can eat in a pergola-shaded courtyard.

✚ E13 ✉ Rio Terrà Antonio Foscarini-Sant'Agnese, Dorsoduro 882 ☎ 041 523 0058 🕐 Closed Thu lunch and Wed ⛴ Accademia 1, 3, 4, 82

AL MASCARON

Pleasant old bar-trattoria with a brisk, informal atmosphere. Venetian fish and seafood cooking is served at brown, heavy wood tables with simple settings and paper table cloths. Beamed ceiling and a line of old black and white photos on the walls. So popular – booking is essential – that the owners have opened the similar Alla Mascareta for wine and snacks a few doors down at 5183.

✚ H11 ✉ Calle Lunga Santa Maria Formosa, Castello 5525 ☎ 041 522 5995 or 041 523 0744 🕐 Both closed Sun; Alla Mascareta open evenings only ⛴ Rialto 1, 3, 4, 82

AI MERCANTI

Situated close to the Rialto's fish market, a perfect location for a restaurant which is devoted mainly to fish and seafood. Tastefully and elegantly decorated, it makes a good alternative if the better-known Alla Madonna (see below) is full. Dishes include *risotto alle vongole* and *spaghetti con melanzane e calamaretti*.

✚ G12 ✉ Calle dei Fusèri, San Marco 4346/a ☎ 041 524 0282 🕐 Closed Sun, Mon lunch and 1–15 Aug ⛴ Rialto 1, 3, 82

AL CONTE PESCAOR

A wonderful tiny fish restaurant that caters to Venetians despite its proximity to Piazza San Marco.

✚ G12 ✉ Piscina San Zulian, San Marco 544 ☎ 041 522 1483 🕐 Closed Sun and Jan ⛴ San Marco 1, 3, 4, 82

ALLA MADONNA

One of Venice's most authentic restaurants and one of the oldest in the city – it has the look and feel of a Venetian restaurant of 20 or 30 years ago. A favourite for business meetings and family celebrations. The good food is rigorously Venetian, including such typical dishes as *sarde in saôr*, *zuppa di pesce* and *ai frutte di mare*. The dining area is roomy and the service efficient, if sometimes brusque.

✚ F11 ✉ Calle della Madonna, San Polo 594 ☎ 041 522 3824 🕐 Closed Wed and two weeks in Aug ⛴ Rialto 1, 3, 82

CORTE SCONTA

Many Venetians and visitors alike rate the Corte Sconta as their favourite among the city's restaurants, despite its slightly peripheral location (close to the Arsenale). It is fairly small (just 70 covers) and is always busy, but nonetheless the atmosphere is pleasant, while the cooking and seafood are rarely less than excellent. There is no menu as such, so try to follow waiting staff's recommendations. However, prices for a full meal have crept up. A small garden is open for outdoor eating in summer. Somewhat hard to find.

✚ J12 ✉ Calle del Pestrin, Castello 3886 ☎ 041 522 7024 ⊘ Closed Sun and Mon ⛴ Arsenale 1

DA ARTURO

Virtually the only fine restaurant in Venice that concentrates on meat dishes rather than fish. Good wine list and a tiny pleasant wood-panelled dining room.

✚ F12 ✉ Rio Terrà degli Assassini, San Marco 3656 ☎ 041 528 6974 ⊘ Closed Sun ⛴ Sant'Angelo 1

DA IGNAZIO

This fairly small and predominantly fish restaurant lies just east of Campo San Tomà, and has the atmosphere of a restaurant from the 1950s. Garden for alfresco dining in summer.

✚ E11 ✉ Calle Saoneri, San Polo 2749 ☎ 041 523 4852 ⊘ Closed Sat and three weeks in Jul and Aug ⛴ San Tomà 1, 82

DA REMIGIO

Neighbourhood trattorias are a dying breed in Venice, so this little restaurant – despite a recent redecoration that has removed some old-fashioned touches – is quite a find. It has just 40 covers, so you will need to book or arrive early to share a table. The food is reliable and homely, the wine list

short but adequate.

✚ J12 ✉ Salizzada dei Greci, Castello 3416 ☎ 041 523 0089 ⊘ Closed Mon evening and Tue ⛴ San Zaccaria or Arsenale 1, 4, 52, 82

FIASCHETTERIA TOSCANA

Despite the 'Toscana' in its name, the menu at this favourite established in 1956 includes classic Venetian dishes and seafood. Excellent selection of wines.

✚ G11 ✉ Salizzada San Giovanni Cristostomo, Cannaregio 5719 ☎ 041 528 5281 ⊘ Closed Tue and three weeks in Jul ⛴ Rialto 1, 3, 82

FIORE

This thoroughly local trattoria has lots of colour, with a popular bar serving snacks as well as an intimate restaurant. Do not confuse it with Da Fiore in San Polo (➤ 68). Just off Campo Santo Stefano (Campo Francesco Morosini).

✚ F12 ✉ Calle delle Botteghe, San Marco 3460 ☎ 041 523 5310 ⊘ Closed Tue ⛴ San Samuele 1

VINI DA GIGIO

A pretty, relaxed and romantic restaurant on a peaceful canal: two simple rooms with beams and old wooden cabinets. Venetian cooking, with fish and meat dishes; short and well-chosen wine list. Good for lunch or dinner.

✚ F10 ✉ Fondamenta della Chiesa-San Felice, Cannaregio 3628/a ☎ 041 528 5140 ⊘ Closed Sun evening, Mon, Jan and three weeks in Aug ⛴ Ca' d'Oro 1

Main courses

Venice's most famous main course is calf's liver and onions (*fegato alla veneziana*), though fish and seafood form the city's main culinary staples. Mussels (*cozze* or *peoci*) from the lagoon are common, together with cuttlefish (*seppie*) and fish such as sole (*sogliola*), red mullet (*triglia*), mullet (*céfalo*), sea bream (*orata*), monkfish (*coda di rospo*) and mackerel (*sgombro*). Fish is best eaten grilled (*alla griglia* or *ai ferri*). For a variety of fish and seafood opt for a *fritto di pesce* or *fritto misto di mare*, a plate of mixed fried fish and seafood. To round off a meal, sample Venice's well-known *tiramisù* (literally 'pick me up'), a liqueur-laced pudding of sponge, mascarpone cheese, eggs and chocolate.

71

BUDGET RESTAURANTS

Paying

The bill (*il conto*) usually includes a cover charge per person (*pane e coperto*) and a 10–15 per cent service charge (*servizio*). Restaurants are required by law to give you a proper receipt (*una ricevuta*). Always check the bill carefully, especially if – as still happens – it is an illegible scrawl on a piece of paper (strictly speaking illegal). Skipping *antipasti* and desserts will reduce costs – go to a *gelateria* for an ice cream instead. Fixed-price tourist menus usually include a basic pasta, main course, fruit and half-bottles of wine and water. Food quality is often indifferent – you will probably find many of the same dishes listed on the menu in a budget trattoria as in the most expensive restaurants. The difference is primarily one of ambience and detail. The *prezzo fisso* menu usually excludes cover, service and beverages. Check what is included in the price.

Remember that cheap snacks and meals are also available in cafés and wine bars (► 74–76).

ACIUGHETA

The 'Little Anchovy' pizzeria-trattoria is one of the best places in the budget price range near Piazza San Marco.
✚ H12 ✉ Campo Santi Filippo e Giacomo, Castello 4357 ☎ 041 522 4292 ◷ Closed Wed in winter 🚤 San Zaccaria 1, 4, 52, 82

AI PROMESSI SPOSI

This friendly bar-restaurant serves up mainly fish dishes that are both cheap and come in huge portions. The bar snacks available are also excellent and even cheaper.
✚ G10 ✉ Calle dell'Oca, Cannaregio 4367 ☎ 041 522 8609 ◷ Closed Wed 🚤 Ca' d'Oro 1

AL GATTO NERO

This traditional trattoria is the best place on Burano for simple, reasonably priced food. Outside tables by the canal overlook the old fish market.
✚ L2 ✉ Calle Stivallo-Fondamenta Giudecca, Burano 88 ☎ 041 730120 ◷ Closed Mon 🚤 Burano 12, 14

ALLA RIVETTA

A cheap but good-quality trattoria close to Piazza San Marco which makes a pleasant alternative to the nearby Aciugheta (see above). It is quite small and often very busy.
✚ H12 ✉ Ponte San Provolo, near Campo Santi Filippo e Giacomo, Castello 4625 ☎ 041 528 7302 ◷ Closed Mon 🚤 San Zaccaria 1, 4, 52, 82

ALLA ZUCCA

Venetians come to this informal trattoria tucked away near San Giacomo dell'Orio when they want a change from Venetian cooking. Dishes are inventive, and often have an Oriental twist. Pleasant service from mostly female staff. Good vegetarian options.
✚ E10 ✉ Ponte del Megio, Santa Croce 1762 ☎ 041 524 1570 ◷ Closed Sun 🚤 San Stae 1

ALLE OCHE

Just south of the quiet little square of Campo San Giacomo dell'Orio. Very popular, so book or arrive early to secure a table outside, and enjoy one of the many pizzas.
✚ E10–E11 ✉ Calle del Tintor, San Polo 1552 ☎ 041 524 1161 ◷ Closed Mon 🚤 Riva di Biasio 1

ANTICO CAPON

A pleasant location on one of Venice's most attractive squares, plus pizzas cooked in a wood-fired oven (a rarity in fire-conscious Venice). In summer rows of tables are laid out on the piazza.
✚ D12 ✉ Campo Santa Margherita, Dorsoduro 3004/b ☎ 041 528 5292 ◷ Closed Wed 🚤 San Tomà or Ca' Rezzonico 1, 82

DONA ONESTA

The 'Honest Woman' lives up to its name, offering good-quality food at budget prices. It is becoming increasingly well-known, however, so try to book ahead to secure a table in its single small dining room. Overlooks a little canal midway between San Pantalon and San Tomà.

✝ E12 ⊠ Calle della Donna Onesta, Dorsoduro ☎ 041 522 9586 🕐 Closed Sun ⛴ San Tomà 1, 82

OSTERIA AI CACCIATORI

A pleasant old-fashioned establishment on Murano's main canal in a street known for its glass shops. One of the few places to eat on the island.

✝ K7–L6 ⊠ Fondamenta dei Vetrai, Murano 69 ⛴ Faro or Colonna 12, 13, 18, 52

ROSTICCERIA SAN BARTOLOMEO

A large self-service place that is good for snacks, especially at lunchtime. There is no cover charge or service downstairs (the restaurant upstairs has almost the same food but at a higher price). Near the Rialto, off Campo San Bartolomeo.

✝ G11 ⊠ Calle della Bissa, San Marco 5424 ☎ 041 522 3569 🕐 Closed Mon ⛴ Rialto 1, 3, 82

TAVERNA SAN TROVASO

Not the best cuisine in the city, yet it offers reliable cooking at reasonable prices. Popular with Venetians, and its location west of the Accademia attracts passing trade. Book to be sure of a place (especially for Sunday lunch).

✝ E13 ⊠ Fondamenta Priuli, Dorsoduro 1016 ☎ 041 520

3703 🕐 Closed Mon ⛴ Accademia 1, 3, 4, 82

TRATTORIA SAN TOMÀ

Both the pizzas and trattoria food served here are good, but this restaurant's best feature is its location on attractive Campo San Tomà, just one minute south of Santa Maria Gloriosa dei Frari and the Scuola Grande di San Rocco.

✝ E12 ⊠ Campo San Tomà, San Polo 2864 ☎ 041 710586 🕐 Closed Tue in winter ⛴ San Tomà 1, 82

VECIO FRITOLIN

A trattoria with old wooden chairs, wonderful glass lamps, ancient mirrors, an age-darkened interior and brown, worn chequered plastic table cloths. Locals crowd in for fine snacks and a handful of main and pasta dishes (largely fish-based) that change daily.

✝ F10–F11 ⊠ Calle della Regina, Santa Croce 2262 ☎ 041 522 2881 🕐 Closed Sun, Mon lunch and Aug ⛴ San Stae 1

VIVALDI

This small relaxed and pleasantly Venetian place produces simple hot dishes that can be eaten informally at the front or sitting down at a few tables to the rear, where more ambitious (and more expensive) meals are also on offer. Or just stop by for a glass of wine.

✝ F11 ⊠ Calle della Madonnetta, San Polo 1457 ☎ 041 523 8185 🕐 Closed Sun ⛴ San Silvestro 1

Drinks

Venice's water is perfectly safe to drink, though Venetians prefer mineral water (*acqua minerale*) – either fizzy (*gassata*) or flat (*liscia, naturale* or *non gassata*). Bottles come in one litre (*un litro* or *una bottiglia*) or half-litre (*mezzo litro* or *mezza bottiglia*) sizes. Bottled fruit juice is *un succo di frutta*, available in pear (*pera*), apricot (*albiccoca*), peach (*pesca*) and other flavours. Fresh juice is *una spremuta*, while milk shake is *un frullato*, or *un frappé* if made with ice cream. *Lemon soda* is a popular and refreshing bitter-lemon drink. Ice is *ghiaccio*, and a slice of lemon is *uno spicchio di limone*.

CAFÉS, BARS & GELATERIE

Etiquette

The procedure when standing up in a bar is to pay for what you want at the cash desk (*la cassa*) and take your receipt (*lo scontrino*) to the bar, where you repeat your order (a L200 tip slapped down on the bar works wonders with the service). Do *not* then take your drink and sit at outside tables, as you almost always pay a premium to sit down when you order through a waiter. Sitting, a single purchase allows you to watch the world go by almost indefinitely. ice cream (*un gelato*) comes in a cone (*un cono*) or a tub (*una coppa*): specify which you want, along with a price (quantity and tub size rise in L500 intervals from about L2,000–4,000). You are also often asked if you want cream (*panna*) on top, which is usually free.

AI VINI PADOVANI

A good, simple and authentic Venetian bar with enthusiastic owners: There is a stand-up counter with a larger room to the right for light meals and snacks.

✚ E12 ✉ Calle dei Cerchieri, Dorsoduro 1280 🚤 Ca' Rezzonico 1

CA' D'ORO

This wonderfully fusty and very Venetian place has been owned by the same family for over a century. Also known as La Vedova ('The Widow'), it serves snacks and basic hot meals.

✚ G10 ✉ Calle del Pistor-Ramo Ca' d'Oro, Cannaregio 3912-3952 🕙 Closed Sun and Thu 🚤 Ca' d'Oro 1

CAFFÈ DEI FRARI

If you do not want to walk to Ciak (see below), try this lively bar just across the bridge in front of Santa Maria Gloriosa dei Frari. A favourite with university students.

✚ E11 ✉ Fondamenta dei Frari, San Polo 2564 🚤 San Tomà 1, 82

CAUSIN

Opened in 1928, this is one of several excellent cafés on Venice's nicest square. Top-quality ice cream and plenty of outdoor tables.

✚ D12 ✉ Campo Santa Margherita, Dorsoduro 2996 🕙 Closed Sat 🚤 Ca' Rezzonico 1

CIAK

Pleasant and relaxed bar after visiting Santa Maria Gloriosa dei Frari and the Scuola Grande di San Rocco. Used by everyone from gondoliers to society ladies. Good lunchtime snacks and sandwiches.

✚ E12 ✉ Campo San Tomà, San Polo 280 🚤 San Tomà 1, 82

FLORIAN

The oldest, prettiest and most expensive of Venice's famous cafés has been serving customers since 1720. Prices are very high, but treat yourself at least once for the experience and the chance to admire the lovely frescoed and mirrored interior.

✚ G12 ✉ Piazza San Marco, San Marco 56–59 🕙 Closed Wed 🚤 San Marco 1, 3, 4, 82

GUANOTTO

A café and ice cream parlour near the Teatro Goldoni that is also allegedly Venice's oldest *pasticceria*, or pastry shop, and is supposed to have invented the spritzer, a mix of white wine, bitters and soda water. Also great for coffee and cocktails.

✚ G12 ✉ Ponte dell' Ovo, San Marco 4819 🕙 Closed Sun in summer 🚤 Rialto, 1, 3, 4, 82

HARRY'S DOLCI

This offshoot of Harry's Bar began as a fancy coffee-shop, but now does meals as well (➤ 69). It remains a good place to treat yourself to a smart morning coffee or afternoon tea in refined but unintimidating surroundings.

✚ D14 ✉ Fondamenta San Biagio, Giudecca 773 ☎ 041 522 4844 🕙 Apr–Oct: daily 10:30AM–3PM, 7:30–10:30PM. Nov–Mar: closed Tue 🚤 Sant'Eufemia 52, 82

IL CAFFÈ

Another appealing and photogenic little bar on Campo Santa Margherita. Its outside tables are a favourite place to soak up the sun and streetlife.

🔒 D12 ✉ Campo Santa Margherita, Dorsoduro 2963 🕐 Closed Sun 🚤 Ca' Rezzonico 1

MARCHINI

This café-*pasticceria* just east of Campo Santo Stefano (Campo Francesco Morosini) is widely regarded as Venice's best. The window displays alone are worth a special visit.

🔒 F12–F13 ✉ Ponte San Maurizio, San Marco 2769 🚤 Santa Maria del Giglio 1

NICO

Organise a walk or stroll in the San Polo or Dorsoduro districts so that you pass this small waterfront bar, renowned for its ice cream, in particular a praline concoction known as *gianduiotto*.

🔒 E14 ✉ Zàttere ai Gesuati, Dorsoduro 922 🕐 Closed Thu 🚤 Zàttere 52, 82

PAOLIN

The best café in one of Venice's nicest squares. Lots of outside tables from which to watch the world go by, and the bonus of some of the city's best ice cream.

🔒 F12 ✉ Campo Santo Stefano (Campo Francesco Morosini), San Marco 2962 🕐 Closed Fri 🚤 Accademia 1, 3, 4, 82

PARADISO PERDUTO

A good choice of bar both day and night if you want to rub shoulders with the more arty and Bohemian of Venice's inhabitants. Lively late at night, plus occasional live music usually on Sundays. Meals and snacks are served at shared wooden tables.

🔒 F9 ✉ Fondamenta della Misericordia, Cannaregio 2540 🕐 Closed Wed 🚤 San Marcuola 1, 82

QUADRI

Not quite so famous or socially exalted as Florian (see opposite) as Quadri was abandoned by Venetian high society in the 19th century because it was frequented by officers of the occupying Austrian army.

🔒 G12 ✉ Piazza San Marco, San Marco 120–4 🕐 Closed Mon 🚤 San Marco 1, 3, 4, 82

ROSA SALVA

Venice's best café chain has outlets city wide. Coffees and cakes are good, but the atmosphere a bit sterile and bland.

🔒 G12 ✉ Campo San Luca, San Marco 🚤 Rialto 1, 3, 82; 🔒 G11–G12 ✉ Merceria San Salvador, San Marco 951 🚤 Rialto 1, 3, 82; 🔒 G12 ✉ Calle Fiubera, San Marco 🚤 San Marco 1, 3, 4, 82

VINO VINO

Rather more showy and smarter than some of Venice's humbler bars, this snug two-roomed spot, close to La Fenice opera house, offers over 100 different wines to accompany its middling snacks and meals.

🔒 F12 ✉ Ponte delle Veste, Calle delle Veste, San Marco 2007/a 🕐 Closed Tue 🚤 Santa Maria del Giglio

Coffee

At breakfast you will be served a milky *cappuccino*, named after the brown robes and white cowls of Capuchin monks. During the rest of the day the locals' coffee of choice is the short, black *espresso* or *un caffè*. A longer *espresso* is a *lungo* or a *doppia* (double). Decaffeinated coffee is *un caffè Hag*, iced coffee *caffè freddo*, and American-style coffee (long and watery) is *un caffè Americano*. Other varieties on offer include *caffè corretto* (with a dash of grappa or brandy), *caffè latte* (a longer *cappuccino*) and *caffè macchiato* (an *espresso* 'stained' with a drop of milk). Note that Italians rarely drink *cappuccino* after midday – and never after a meal, when they opt for *espresso* or camomile tea (*una camomila*) instead.

75

WINE BARS

Wine bars

Old-fashioned wine bars, or *bacari*, are a Venetian way of life. One of the city's more civilised habits is the custom of breaking up the day with an *ombra* ('shadow'), a small glass of wine that takes its name from the idea of escaping the heat of the sun for a restorative tipple. A small snack, or *cichetto*, usually accompanies the drink. An *enoteca* is a more refined bar, with a greater choice of wines and a range of reasonably priced snacks and hot meals.

AL VOLTO

A genuine dark, wood-beamed *enoteca* north of Campo Manin. Good snacks and a staggering 1,300 wines from Italy and the rest of the world.

✚ F12 ⊠ Calle Cavalli, San Marco 4081 Ⓒ Closed Sun 🚊 Rialto 1, 3, 82

ANTICO DOLO

The Rialto market district has one of the city's largest selections of old-fashioned wine bars. This, along with the nearby Do Mori (see below), is one of the best. Excellent snacks and a small, but fine menu for evening meals.

✚ F11 ⊠ Ruga Vecchia San Giovanni, San Polo 778 Ⓒ Closed Sun 🚊 Rialto 1, 3, 82

BOLDRIN

Excellent and spacious *enoteca* in the northern part of the city. Wine by the glass and hot snacks. Wonderfully mixed clientele – old ladies with little dogs to paint-spattered builders.

✚ G11 ⊠ Salizzada San Chianciano, Cannaregio 5550 Ⓒ Closed Sun 🚊 Rialto 1, 3, 82

CANTINA DEL VINO GIÀ SCHIAVI

An old-fashioned wine bar that really looks the part, set almost opposite San Trovaso and one of Venice's few remaining gondola workshops.

✚ E13 ⊠ Fondamenta Nani-Meravegie, Dorsoduro 992 Ⓒ Closed Sun 🚊 Accademia, Zàttere 1, 3, 4, 82

DO MORI

The most authentic and atmospheric of Venice's old-time *bacari*, in business since 1462. Always filled with locals, shoppers and traders from the nearby Rialto markets. Good snacks; 350 wines. No seats or tables.

✚ F11 ⊠ Calle do Mori, off Ruga Vecchia San Giovanni, San Polo 429 Ⓒ Closed Sun, Wed afternoon 🚊 Rialto 1, 3, 82

DO SPADE

Do Spade is not quite as hectic and nicely down-at-heel as the nearby Do Mori (see above), but is almost as busy and equally authentic. Unlike its neighbour, it also has tables. Difficult to find.

✚ F11 ⊠ Sottoponego Spade, off Calle Angelo, San Polo 860 Ⓒ Jul–Aug: Mon–Wed, Fri–Sat 9–2, 5–8; Thu 9–2. Sep–Jun: Mon–Wed, Fri–Sat 9–2, 5–11; Thu 9–2. Closed Sun 🚊 Rialto 1, 3, 82

OSTERIA AGLI ASSASSINI

Wine bar off the beaten track between Campo Manin and Campo Sant'Angelo with a good selection of wines, light snacks and basic meals.

✚ F12 ⊠ Rio Terrà degli Assassini, San Marco 3695 Ⓒ Closed Sat lunch and Sun 🚊 Sant'Angelo 1

OSTERIA ALLE BOTTEGHE

Lively and very busy wine bar, just north of Campo Santo Stefano (Campo Francesco Morosini). Plenty of wines and a small selection of snacks.

✚ F12 ⊠ Calle delle Botteghe, San Marco Ⓒ Closed Sun 🚊 Sant'Angelo or San Samuele 1, 3, 4, 82

GLASS & BEADS

ANTICLEA ANTQUARIATO

This beautiful little shop is an absolute treasure trove of antique Venetian beads and jewellery. The owner has spent a lifetime amassing her stock, the best of which is kept in countless small drawers around the walls. Beads of your choice can be made up on the spot into earrings or necklaces.

✚ H12 ✉ Campo San Provolo, Castello 4719/a ☎ 041 528 6946 🚤 San Zaccaria 1, 4, 52, 82

BAROVIER E TOSO

One of the better of the many glass showrooms on Murano, this family firm dates back to the 14th century and makes glass to traditional designs, drawing its inspiration from a private 26,000-piece collection of antique glass.

✚ K7–L6 ✉ Fondamenta dei Vetrai, Murano 28 ☎ 041 739049 🚤 Colonna or Faro 12, 52

L'ISOLA

Grotesque modern glass litters countless Venetian shops and souvenir stands. This shop has some of the city's better contemporary designs, although you may still find some of them too far-fetched. As with much Venetian glass, prices can be surprisingly high.

✚ G12 ✉ Salizzada San Moisè, San Marco 1468 ☎ 041 523 1973 🚤 San Marco 1, 3, 4, 82

PAULY

Pauly has been selling the finest Venetian glass since 1866. Its warren of showrooms contain all manner of treasures, including antique pieces that can be copied to order. A little over half-a-million dollars will buy you the company's finest chandelier.

✚ K12 ✉ Ponte Consorzi, Calle Larga, Castello 4391 ☎ 041 520 9899 🚤 San Zaccaria 1, 4, 52, 82

SALVIATI

Founded in 1866, Salviati is known for having provided the eye-catching mosaics on the façade of the Grand Canal's Palazzo Salviati, on the south bank close to the Palazzo Dario. Outlets in Murano and in Venice proper.

✚ F13 ✉ Campo Santa Maria Zobenigo, San Marco 2461 ☎ 041 522 4033 🚤 Santa Maria del Giglio 1

SEGUSO

Another of Murano's better and more established institutions, Seguso has been in business for several decades. Renowned for its copies of antique glass.

✚ L6 ✉ Fondamenta dei Vetrai, Murano 143 ☎ 041 739423 🚤 Colonna or Faro 12, 52

VENINI

Venini has been a Murano institution since the 1930s, attracting some of the top names in glass design. Designs are more up-market and daring than those of many producers.

✚ G12 ✉ Piazzetta dei Leoni (Piazzetta dei Leoncini), San Marco 314 ☎ 041 277 0389 🚤 San Marco 1, 3, 4, 82; ✚ K7–L6 ✉ Fondamenta dei Vetrai, Murano 50 ☎ 041 527 4870 or 041 739955 🚤 Colonna, Faro or Museo 12, 52

Poison daggers

Murano glass was said to be so fine that it would shatter on coming into contact with even the smallest drop of poison. It was also used in the Venetian dagger, one of the Middle Ages' nastiest weapons. Much loved by Venice's secret police, the dagger consisted of a razor-sharp blade of glass, sheathed in metal, which when sunk into a victim's body would snap off at the haft. The unfortunate's skin would close over the glass, leaving a wound apparently no more than an innocent graze at the point of entry.

WINDOW-SHOPPING

Where to look

Fine shops can be found across Venice, but the city's better and more up-market shops (especially for shoes and fashion) cluster in well-defined areas such as the Calle dei Fabbri (⊞ G12); Calle dell'Ascensione-Calle Larga (Viale) XXII Marzo (⊞ F13–G12); the Frezzeria (⊞ G12); and the so-called Mercerie – San Zulian, d'Orologio and San Salvador – which run from Piazza San Marco to the Rialto (⊞ G12).

Department stores

The only large department store worthy of the name is the excellent COIN, which sells a wide range of fashion, toiletries, accessories, china, linen, gifts and general goods. It occupies a large corner block on the east side of Salizzada San Giovanni Crisostomo between the Rialto and the church of San Giovanni Crisostomo (⊞ G11).

EMILIO CECCATO

If there is one souvenir, over and above glass, that greets you at every turn in Venice, it is the fake gondolier's straw hat. This unique little shop sells the genuine article, together with gondoliers' garb – hats, tunics and trousers – to both gondoliers and curious foreigners.
⊞ G11 ⊠ Sottoportico di Rialto, San Polo 1617 ☎ 041 522 2700 ⊞ Rialto 1, 3, 82

EMPORIO ARMANI

No leading Italian city would be complete without a flagship store dedicated to one of the most famous names in Italian fashion. In Venice, Armani's is in one of the city's main shopping streets, a short walk from Piazza San Marco. The clothes are peerless, classic and exquisitely cut.
⊞ G12 ⊠ Calle dei Fabbri, San Marco 989 ☎ 041 523 7808 ⊞ Rialto 1, 3, 82

FIORELLA

Hilarious and wonderfully original, Fiorella has Venice's best-dressed window: the shop dummies, crafted in wood, represent life-sized models of former doges, each incongruously decked out in high heels and other slightly off-beat high fashion items.
⊞ F12 ⊠ Campo Santo Stefano (Campo Francesco Morosini), San Marco 2806 ☎ 041 520 9228 ⊞ Accademia 1, 3, 4, 82

JESURUM

Factory-made lace has undercut and largely supplanted the famous traditional hand-made speciality from Burano (➤ 20). Original and old-style lace is now extremely rare and expensive. This shop, close to the Rialto bridge, has an excellent selection of both types, plus a fine collection of superb linens and lingerie. Other little shops selling lace, often at keen prices, are dotted around the city. Place-settings and similar small pieces make excellent gifts.
⊞ G11 ⊠ Merceria del Capitello, San Marco 4857 ☎ 041 520 6177 ⊞ Rialto 1, 3, 82

LABORATORIO ARTIGIANO MASCHERE

This wonderful mask workshop, located just east of Santi Giovanni e Paolo, is home to Giorgio Clanetti, scion of a family of puppet-makers, who was one of the first to resurrect the Venetian mask-making tradition. Also other paper-mâché objects such as boxes, frames and pots.
⊞ H11–J11 ⊠ Barbaria delle Tole, Castello 6637 ☎ 041 522 3110 ⊞ Ospedale 23, 52

LAURA BIAGIOTTA

One of the big names in Italian high fashion, in the heart of one of the city's most exclusive shopping streets, which runs west from Piazza San Marco.
⊞ F13–G12 ⊠ Calle Larga (Viale) XXII Marzo, San Marco 2400/a ☎ 041 520 3401 ⊞ San Marco 1, 3, 4, 82

MARFORIO

Founded in 1875 and run by the same family for five

generations, this store claims to be Italy's oldest and largest retailer of leather goods. Quality and range are both excellent, with bags, accessories and other leather goods from all the top names in the fashion firmament.

✚ G11 ✉ Campo San Salvador, San Marco 5033 ☎ 041 522 5734 💳 Rialto 1, 3, 4, 82

MISSIAGLIA

Missiaglia's superlative gold and silver jewellery means it is widely considered the city's finest jeweller. White and yellow gold settings with coloured stones are the main speciality: styles are mostly classic, but with occasional more contemporary pieces. With a Piazza San Marco setting, bargains are few and far between.

✚ G12 ✉ Procuratie Vecchie, Piazza San Marco 125 ☎ 041 522 4464 💳 San Marco 1, 3, 4, 82

MISSONI

Another of the big Italian fashion names, best known for highly coloured knitwear and similarly innovative linens, bedwear and casualwear.

✚ G12–G13 ✉ Calle Vallaresso, San Marco 1312 ☎ 041 520 5733 💳 San Marco 1, 3, 4, 82

MONDO NOVO

The masks in this attractive shop just south of Campo Santa Margherita are definitely superior to the mediocre versions in lesser shops around the city. A wonderful place for children and adults alike.

✚ D12 ✉ Rio Terrà Canal, Dorsoduro 3063 ☎ 041 528 7344 💳 Ca' Rezzonico 1

NARDI

Rivals Missiaglia (see opposite) for the title of Venice's smartest jeweller. High prices.

✚ G12 ✉ Procuratie Nuove, Piazza San Marco 69 ☎ 041 522 5733 💳 San Marco 1, 3, 4, 82

RUBELLI

Rubelli has been turning out stunning traditional fabrics since 1850. As many of its skilled workers are retiring there is talk of transforming the workshop into a museum.

✚ F12 ✉ Palazzo Corner Spinelli, Calle dell'Albero, Sant'Angelo, San Marco 3877 ☎ 041 521 6411 💳 Sant'Angelo 1

VALENTINO

The doyen of Rome *alta moda* and stylish ready-to-wear clothes has a shop just west of Piazza San Marco close to the stores of other leading names in the world of high fashion.

✚ G12 ✉ Salizzada San Moisè, San Marco 1473 ☎ 041 520 5733 💳 San Marco 1, 3, 4, 82

VENEZIARTIGIANA

A perfect place to shop for gifts, this store collects the varied work of numerous local craftspeople under one roof: choose from masks, silverware, jewellery, ceramics, creations in wood, pictures, posters and a host of other beautiful objects.

✚ F13–G12 ✉ Calle Larga (Viale) XXII Marzo, San Marco 412–13 💳 San Marco or Santa Maria del Giglio 1, 3, 4, 82

Mariano Fortuny

Fortuny was born in Catalonia (Spain) in 1871, the son of a painter and fabric-collector. He moved to Venice when he was 18, soon gaining renown in fields ranging from physics and chemistry to architecture and theatre design. Today, he is best remembered for his fabrics, and in particular for the pleated dresses he created that were so fine they could be rolled up and threaded through a wedding ring. Sadly, none of his famous dresses feature amongst the interesting and unusual items on display in the Museo Fortuny. ✚ F12

✉ Palazzo Pesaro, Campo San Benedetto, San Marco 3780

🕐 Tue–Sun 9–7

💳 Sant'Angelo 1 💵 Expensive

79

BOOKS, PAPER & STATIONERY

Antiques

Bric-a-brac and antique bargains are rare in a city that is acutely aware of its past and the value of its objets d'art. Still Venice offers an almost unlimited choice of beautiful things to buy. Antique shops are dotted around the city; but the largest concentrations are found around San Maurizio and Santa Maria Zobenigo just east of Campo Santo Stefano (Campo Francesco Morosini ✠ F12–F13). Slightly cheaper shops can be found in the area around San Barnaba (✠ D12). The most famous shops are Paolo Scarpa's two outlets at Campo San Moisè, San Marco 1464 (✠ G12), and Calle Larga (Viale) XXII Marzo, San Marco 2089 (✠ F13–G12). Regular flea and antique markets are held in Campo San Maurizio; contact the tourist office for dates.

ALBERTO VALESE

Valese was at the cutting edge of the 1970s revival in traditional Venetian marbled paper. This is his workshop, which is open to visitors. He has another outlet for his marbled paper, fabrics and ornaments (see also Ebrû below).
✠ F12 ✉ Salizzada San Samuele, San Marco 3331 ☎ 041 520 0921 🚤 Sant'Angelo or Accademia 1, 3, 4, 82

EBRÛ

Alberto Valese's main shop takes its name from the traditional Turkish marbling technique used to create many of his products. Some of the smaller items make ideal gifts or souvenirs to take home.
✠ F12 ✉ Campo Santo Stefano, San Marco 3471 ☎ 041 523 8830 🚤 Santa Maria del Giglio 1

FANTONI

This well-known shop contains the city's largest selection of big, glossy art books.
✠ F12–G12 ✉ Salizzada San Luca, San Marco 4119 ☎ 041 522 0700 🚤 Rialto 1, 3, 82

FILIPPI EDITORE VENEZIA

This specialist shop is renowned for its large collection of books on all aspects of Venice (mostly in Italian) and its many facsimile editions of old books.
✠ G11 ✉ Calle della Casselleria, San Marco 5284 ☎ 041 523 6916 🚤 Rialto 1, 3, 82

GOLDONI

This well-stocked shop is by common consent the best general bookstore in the city. It has a wide range of literature on the city, along with a limited selection of English and other foreign-language titles.
✠ G12 ✉ Calle dei Fabbri, San Marco 4742 ☎ 041 522 2384 🚤 San Marco 1, 3, 4, 82

LEGATORIA PIAZZESI

Established in 1900, this is one of the last workshops in Venice to use traditional wood-block methods to hand-print its papers, books and stationery. Its beautiful products are expensive.
✠ F12 ✉ Campiello della Feltrina, San Marco 2511 ☎ 041 522 1202 🚤 Santa Maria del Giglio 1

PAOLO OLBI

Another artisan at the forefront of the marbled paper revival. Olbi's appealing shop sells a wide range of marbled stationery and ornaments.
✠ F12 ✉ Calle della Mandola, San Marco 3653 ☎ 041 528 5025 🚤 Sant'Angelo 1

POLLIERO

A tiny, old-fashioned shop standing alongside Santa Maria Gloriosa dei Frari, Polliero sells a lovely selection of leather-bound and marbled paper stationery, together with hand-made gifts and beautiful individual sheets of paper.
✠ E11 ✉ Campo dei Frari, San Polo 2995 ☎ 041 528 5130 🚤 San Tomà 1, 82

FOOD & DRINK

ALIANI (CASA DEL PARMIGIANO)

Perhaps Venice's most famous delicatessen, this shop has a superlative selection of cheeses, together with a variety of hams, salamis, fresh pasta and other ready-made delicacies.

⊞ F11 ✉ Campo della Corderia, Ruga Vecchia San Giovanni, San Polo 214 ☎ 041 520 6525 ⛴ Rialto or San Silvestro 1, 3, 82

ERBERIA

Venice's main outdoor market provides a wonderful spectacle of sound and colour, its stalls laden with fruit and vegetables, its thoroughfares busy with shoppers and traders. Be sure to explore the maze of stalls north of Campo San Giacomo di Rialto, not merely the more touristy stalls that line the Ruga degli Orefici.

⊞ G11 ✉ Campo San Giacomo di Rialto ◷ Mon–Sat 7–1 ⛴ Rialto 1, 3, 82

MARKETS

Market stalls can be found in the following locations: Campo Santa Margherita (⊞ D12); Campo Santa Maria Formosa (⊞ H11); Campiello dell'Anconetta-Rio Terrà San Leonardo (⊞ E9); the boats moored on Rio della Tana (⊞ K13–L13); and, most evocatively, the famous covered barge by the Ponte dei Pugni on Fondamenta Gerardini (⊞ D12).

MASCARI

A specialist food shop near the Rialto known for its

teas, coffees, seeds and dried goods.

⊞ F11 ✉ Ruga dei Spezieri, San Polo 380 ☎ 041 522 9762 ⛴ Rialto or San Silvestro 1, 3, 82

PASTICCERIA MARCHINI

Delicious cakes, biscuits, pastries and sweetmeats from Venice's finest *pasticceria*.

⊞ F13 ✉ Ponte San Maurizio, San Marco 2769 ☎ 041 522 9109 ⛴ Santa Maria del Giglio 1

PESCHERIA

Venice's evocative fish market, its stalls loaded with all manner of exotic-looking fish and seafood, merges seamlessly with the fruit and vegetable stalls of the adjoining Erberia (see opposite).

⊞ F11–G11 ✉ Campo della Pescaria ◷ Tue–Sat 7–1 ⛴ Rialto 1, 3, 82

WINE

Old-fashioned wine shops, where you can take empty bottles to be filled from wooden barrels or wicker-wrapped vats, still dot most Venetian neighbourhoods. The wine – which can also be bought in bottles – is good and cheap, and embraces most of the Veneto's many varieties of red and white, including some that are hard to find elsewhere. Wine bars also sell wine by the bottle to take away (➤ 76). The following La Nave d'Oro outlets are typical:

⊞ D12 ✉ Campo Santa Margherita, Dorsoduro 3664; ⊞ H11 ✉ Calle del Mondo Novo, Castello 5786; ⊞ E9 ✉ Rio Terrà San Leonardo, Cannaregio 1370

Practicalities

Food shops and bakeries are usually open 8:30–1 and 4–7, though virtually all close on Wednesday afternoons and Sundays. Food served by weight (including bread) is sold by the *chilo*, *mezzo chilo* (kilo and half-kilo) and, more commonly, by the *etto* (100g), plural *etti*.

The Rialto

As a district the Rialto is almost as old as the city itself, the earliest settlers having been attracted to its high banks, or *rivo alto*, these forming a dry and easily defended redoubt amidst the marsh and mud of the lagoon. While San Marco developed into the city's political heart, the Rivoaltus became its commercial centre, where all manner of staple and exotic goods were traded in the 'Bazaar of Europe'. The first private banks appeared here in 1157, these soon followed (in 1161) by the Banco di Piazza, Europe's state bank. It did not take long for the tax collectors, magistrates and other offices of state to appear in their wake.

AFTER DARK

What's on

Details of films, concerts and exhibitions in Venice can be found in the '*Spettacoli*' section of daily editions of local newspapers such as *Il Gazzettino* and *La Nuova Venezia*. *Un Ospite di Venezia*, a free Italian/English magazine available from hotels and tourist offices, also contains detailed listings (published weekly in high season, monthly in low season). Tourist offices always have plenty of posters and leaflets on current events. Also keep an eye open for posters on the streets.

CASINÒ

Venice's popular Casinò Municipale (Municipal Casino), one of only a handful in Italy, is housed in winter in the Palazzo Vendramin-Calergi, one of the Grand Canal's most impressive palaces. From mid-June until mid-September it moves to the Lido at the Palazzo del Casinò. Dress smartly and take along your passport.
🔲 F9–F10 ✉ Palazzo Vendramin-Calergi, Calle Larga Vendramin, off Rio Terrà della Maddalena, Cannaregio ☎ 041 710211 🕐 Mid-Sep–mid-Jun: daily 4PM–2:30AM 🚢 San Marcuola 1, 82 ❓ Dress code: smart; 🔲 J17–K17
✉ Palazzo del Casinò, Piazzale del Casinò, Lungomare G Marconi, Lido ☎ 041 529 7111
🕐 Mid-Jun–mid-Sep: daily 4PM–2:30AM 🚢 Casinò or Santa Maria Elisabetta 1, 6, 40, 41, 52, 82 ❓ Dress code: smart

CINEMA

Considering the fact that Venice hosts one of Europe's leading film festivals, it seems astonishing that it has just five cinemas. Art-house, classic or original-language films are screened occasionally at the so-called Cinema d'Essai, but virtually all foreign and current-release films are dubbed into Italian. The city's principal cinemas are listed below.
Accademia 🔲 E13 ✉ Calle Corfù, Dorsoduro 1018 ☎ 041 528 7706 🚢 Accademia 1, 3, 4, 82; **Centrale** 🔲 G12
✉ Piscina da Frezzeria, San Marco 1659 ☎ 041 522 8201 🚢 San Marco 1, 3, 4, 82;
Olimpia 🔲 G12 ✉ Campo

San Gallo o Canova, San Marco 1094 ☎ 041 520 5439 🚢 San Marco 1, 3, 4, 82; **Ritz** 🔲 G12 ✉ Calle dei Segretaria, near Campo San Zulian, San Marco 617 ☎ 041 520 4429 🚢 San Marco 1, 3, 4, 82; **Rossini** 🔲 E12 ✉ Calle delle Muneghe, San Marco 4000 ☎ 041 523 0322 🚢 San Samuele 3, 4, 82

CLASSICAL MUSIC

Venice's main classical music venue is La Fenice (see 'Opera' ► 83), a lovely building which, until it was gutted by fire, presented a winter opera season and a summer season of miscellaneous classical concerts. In its (temporary) absence the city's main classical music venue is La Pietà, Vivaldi's former church, which presents regular concerts of the Venetian composer's work plus other occasional recitals. Tickets are rather expensive, and often pricier than the performance merits. Concerts are also held in the churches of San Stae, Santo Stefano and Santa Maria Gloriosa dei Frari, San Barnaba and the Ospedaletto, and at the Palazzo Prigione Vecchie, the Palasport dell'Arsenale and the Scuola Grande di San Giovanni Evangelista. Keep your eyes open for posters advertising concerts, or enquire at the tourist office regarding forthcoming events (► 87).

The state radio network, RAI, allows the public into recordings of its concerts in the Palazzo

Labia, though the free tickets must be reserved in advance (see below). Several small foundations also organise occasional recitals, most notably the Cini Foundation, based at San Giorgio Maggiore, and the Ugo and Olga Levi Foundation, based at the Palazzo Giustinian-Lolin (enquire at the tourist office for details). The Amici della Musica is a 'club' next to the Miracoli church which holds small concerts, art exhibitions, and nightly readings of prose and poetry.

Amici della Musica ⊞ G11 ✉ Campo Miracoli ☎ 041 528 7986 🚊 Rialto 1, 3, 82;

La Pietà (Santa Maria della Pietà o della Visitazione) ⊞ H12 ✉ Riva degli Schiavoni ☎ 041 523 1096 🚊 San Zaccaria 1, 4, 52, 82 ❓ Tickets expensive;

RAI ⊞ E9 ✉ Palazzo Labia, Campo San Geremia ☎ 041 716666 🚊 Ferrovia 1, 3, 4, 52, 82

CLUBS

Venice has a reputation as a rather sleepy place, and young Venetians often complain about its lack of nightlife. The majority of the region's big discos and clubs are in Mestre and distant Jesolo on the mainland (see newspaper listings for details), while the closest any big bands get to the city for concerts is Padua or Verona. Venice's only 'disco' is the rather unhip Club El Souk (see below). Livelier and more fashionable are Round Midnight, a bar-club with dancing, and the atmospheric Paradiso Perduto, a bar-restaurant

with occasional live music. Harry's Dolci, on the Giudecca, is a smart café-restaurant that has occasional jazz concerts. (See listings below).

Harry's Dolci ⊞ D14 ✉ Fondamenta San Biagio, Giudecca 773 ☎ 041 522 4844 🕔 Apr–Oct: daily 10:30AM–3PM, 7:30–10:30PM. Nov–Mar: closed Tue 🚊 Sant'Eufemia 52, 82;

Club El Souk ⊞ E13 ✉ Calle Corfù, Dorsoduro 1056/a ☎ 041 520 0371 🕔 Bar: 10AM–8PM. Disco: 10PM–4AM 🚊 Accademia 1, 3, 4, 82;

Paradiso Perduto ⊞ F9 ✉ Fondamenta della Misericordia, Cannaregio 2540 ☎ 041 720581 🕔 Closed Wed 🚊 San Marcuola or Madonna dell' Orto 1, 52, 82;

Round Midnight ⊞ E13 ✉ Fondamenta dello Squero, Dorsoduro 3102 ☎ 041 523 1078 🕔 Nightly except Wed 🚊 Ca' Rezzonico 1

OPERA

The catastrophic fire at La Fenice ('The Phoenix') has put Venice's famous opera house out of action for the foreseeable future. Plans to rebuild and restore its once magnificent interior are well advanced, though it is almost impossible to know when the hall will finally reopen for performances. In the meantime, temporary venues have been arranged for opera performances. The main place is the Palafenice on the Isola Nuova del Tronchetto.

⊞ F12 ✉ Teatro La Fenice, Campo San Fantin, San Marco 1965 ☎ 041 521 0161 or 041 520 4010; fax 041 522 1768

Evening pastimes

Venice does not have the nightlife to match other major cities. For many Venetians an evening out consists of a meal or drink with friends rounded off with a stroll to a bar for a coffee or ice cream. One of the best places to join them is Campo Santa Margherita, a square full of easy-going bars and cafés in the student district of Dorsoduro (⊞ D12). Other similar squares include Campo San Polo (⊞ E11–F11), Campo Santo Stefano (Campo Francesco Morosini ⊞ F12), Campo San Barnaba (⊞ D12) and Campo Santa Maria Formosa (⊞ H11). Indeed, few cities can compare with Venice when it comes to atmospheric evening strolls. Certainly none can offer the experience of a gondola or *vaporetto* ride on the Grand Canal.

FESTIVALS

Regata Storica

The Regata Storica ('Historic Regatta'; first Sunday in September) is the most famous of several annual regattas held in and around the city each year. A huge flotilla of beautifully decorated craft, their crews in period dress, travels in colourful procession down the Grand Canal (note that onlookers are expected to dress the part too). Races are then held, the most exciting being those between rival gondoliers.

Marriage to the Sea

This ceremony began around AD 1000 when Doge Pietro Orseolo II set sail to attack Dalmatia, among the first of Venice's conquests. Originally a libation before battle, in time it came to symbolise the Republic's naval power and special relationship with the sea. The doge and his retinue would sail into the lagoon, there dropping a golden ring into the water and reciting the words: 'We espouse thee, O sea, in sign of our real and perpetual dominion over thee.' Divers then competed to find the ring, the winner – if any – earning relief from 'all the burdens to which dwellers in the Republic are subject'.

CARNIVAL

Venice's famous carnival takes its name from the Latin *carnem levare*, or *carne vale* – the 'farewell to meat'. It probably began in the city's 15th-century private clubs, whose members indicated their allegiances by wearing different coloured hose. Although the clubs initially limited themselves to boat races and social frivolities, they eventually took to competing in masked balls on Martedì Grasso, the prelude to Lent. Resurrected as recently as 1979 (by a group of non-Venetians), it emulates the great pre-Lenten festivals of the 18th century, thousands of tourists dressing in masks and extravagant costumes to indulge in a series of enthusiastically supported events. Today, the carnival officially lasts just ten days (up to the beginning of Lent), though the event has become so large – and so commercialised – that Venice often has to be 'shut' for the duration.

FESTA DEL REDENTORE

The Festa del Redentore is the more spectacular of the two major festivals held to celebrate Venice's deliverance from past epidemics (the other is the Festa della Salute; see below). Observed on the third Sunday of July, it commemorates the end of the 1576 plague, an epidemic that wiped out a third of the city's inhabitants. In times past the doge and his entourage would visit the church of the Redentore, crossing to the Giudecca on a pontoon of boats thrown across the Canale della Giudecca. Today, Venetians stream across a similar bridge on the Saturday evening, many taking to boats for a traditional picnic on the water.

FESTA DELLA SALUTE

Like the Festa del Redentore, the feast of La Salute (21 November) commemorates Venice's deliverance from bubonic plague, in this case the epidemic of 1630 which claimed an estimated one-third of the city's population. Ever since, Venetians have crossed a pontoon bridge thrown across the Grand Canal to Santa Maria della Salute (built to mark the end of the plague; ▶ 34), to offer thanks for their health (*salute*) and to pray for sick friends and relations.

LA SENSA

The feast of the La Sensa (Sunday after Ascension Day) is a resurrected version of the ancient Marriage to the Sea ceremony (see panel). The city mayor, his retinue and assorted VIPs sail out onto the lagoon on a copy of the *Bucintoro*, the old dogal state barge. Also in May is the more impressive Vogalonga, or 'Long Row', during which boats compete in a 32km race to the island of Burano and back.

VENICE
travel facts

ARRIVING & DEPARTING

Before you go

- EU, Commonwealth and US citizens require a passport for visits to Italy.
- Visas are usually required for nationals of other countries.

When to go

- Try to avoid July and August, the hottest and busiest months, and plan a visit for April, May, June, September or October.
- Hotels are busy from Easter to October, in February during Carnevale, and over Christmas and New Year.
- Despite the weather, winter can still be a delightful time to see the city.

Climate

- Venice has generally mild winters and warm summers, but the latter can be hot and oppressive, with occasional thunderstorms (especially in September), while winter temperatures often match those of northern European cities. A chill easterly wind, the *bora*, can lower temperatures in spring and autumn.
- Outside the summer months, fog is common.
- Flooding (*acqua alta*) can occur any time, but especially between November and March.

Arriving by air

- Scheduled internal and international flights (plus a few charters) arrive at Venice's Marco Polo Airport, 9km north of the city centre ☎ 041 260 9260/6111.
- Most charters arrive at Treviso, 30km from Venice. A shuttlebus runs to Treviso town centre, from where there are regular bus and train connections to Venice.
- Connections from Marco Polo to Venice's Piazzale Roma (between 20–40 minutes) can be made by taxi, by blue ATVO buses, or by the cheaper and less-frequent ACTV No. 5 orange city buses. Tickets for buses must be bought before boarding from the office inside the arrivals terminal. Buses depart from the concourse outside the terminal. You can also take a water taxi to most points within the city (20 minutes) but the prices are high (over L100,000). A cheaper public water launch makes the journey (50 minutes) to San Marco, the Lido and Záttere. Tickets are available from an office close to the arrivals terminal exit; the quay is immediately outside.

Arriving by train

- Trains to Venice arrive at Venezia Santa Lucia station, often abbreviated to Venezia SL ☎ 041 715555.
- The station is located at the head of the Grand Canal, five minutes' walk from Piazzale Roma, and has frequent *vaporetto* (1, 3, 4, 82) and *motoscafo* (52) boat services to the rest of the city from the quays outside. Be sure the boat is heading in the right direction.
- Note that many through trains stop on the mainland at Mestre station, confusingly called Venezia Mestre (Venezia M), without continuing to Venice proper. Check your train is destined for Santa Lucia; if not, catch one of the frequent connecting services at Mestre for the 15-minute trip across the causeway.

Arriving by car

- Cars *must* be left at one of the multi-storey car parks at the Tronchetto (linked by boat 82 to the rest of the city) or the more central Piazzale Roma, from where you can walk or catch boats 1, 3, 4, 52 or 82. Rates start at about L15,000 a day. There are *no* free car parks and no other parking places (cars will be towed away).

• Summer queues on the causeway approaching the city are common. You might consider leaving cars in Mestre and then taking a train (see above).

Customs regulations

• Limits on most tax-paid goods (goods bought in ordinary shops) within the EU were dropped on 1 January 1993. Duty-free limits are as follows: 800 cigarettes plus 400 cigarillos plus 1kg tobacco plus 200 cigars; 10 litres of spirits or 20 litres of fortified wine plus 90 litres of wine (not more than 60 per cent sparkling) plus 110 litres of beer.

ESSENTIAL FACTS

Local tourist information:

• Main tourist offices ✚ G13
✉ Palazzetto Selva (white building on the waterfront on the west side of the Giardinetti Reali), Fondamenta delle Farine ☎ 041 522 6356; fax 041 529 8730; ✚ G12 ✉ Piazza San Marco, 71/c (Ascensione) ☎ 041 529 8730; fax 041 529 8730 ⏰ Summer: Mon–Sat 9:10–6:50. Winter: Mon–Sat 9:30–3:30

• Train station office ✚ D10 ☎ 041 529 8711/8727; hotel booking agency 041 715016 or 041 715288 ⏰ 8AM–9PM

• Marco Polo Airport office ✚ off map ☎ 041 541 5887 ⏰ Summer: 9–1, 2–6. Winter: 9:30–3:30

• Lido office ✚ L16 ✉ Gran Viale Santa Maria Elisabetta 6 ☎ 041 526 5721 ⏰ Summer: 8:30–7:30. Winter: 9:30–3:30

Travel insurance

• A fully comprehensive travel insurance policy is highly recommended.

Opening hours

• Banks: Mon–Fri 8–1:30 (larger branches also 3–4).

• Churches: No fixed hours, but generally Mon–Sat 9–noon, 3–6; Sun 2–5; except Basilica di San Marco: 9:45–5.

• Museums: Varied, but state-run galleries generally Tue–Sat 9–2; Sun 9–1; city-run and private museums such as the Correr, Palazzo Ducale and Guggenheim usually open all day.

• Parks: 9–one hour before sunset.

• Post offices: Mon–Sat 8–1:30, though small offices may not open on Sat, while main offices remain open 8–7 for some services.

• Restaurants: Many close on Sun evening and all day Mon, plus a statutory closing day once a week (*la chiusura settimanale*).

• Shops and offices: Generally 9–1, 4–8; most food shops close Wed afternoons except in summer, while other shops close Mon mornings except in summer.

National holidays

• 1 Jan: New Year's Day
• 6 Jan: Epiphany
• Easter Sunday
• Easter Monday
• 25 Apr: Liberation Day
• 1 May: Labour Day
• 15 Aug: Assumption
• 1 Nov: All Saints' Day
• 8 Dec: Immaculate Conception
• Christmas Day
• 26 Dec: Santo Stefano
• 21 Nov: Shops and businesses may also close or observe shorter hours during the Festa della Salute
• Good Friday is not a holiday

Money matters

• The unit of Italian currency is the lira (plural lire), abbreviated to L.
• Currency is issued in denominations

of: (notes) L1,000, L2,000, L5,000, L10,000, L50,000 and L100,000; (coins) L5 and L10 (both rare), L50, L100, L200, L500 and L1000.

- Note that there are two new small L50 and L100 coins, both still in circulation with the older and larger coins.
- The euro became the official currency of Italy on 1 January 1999, and the lira became a denomination of the euro. Lira notes and coins continue to be legal tender until euro bank notes and coins are introduced on 1 January 2002.
- The L200 telephone token (*gettone*) can be used as a coin.
- Foreign-exchange facilities (*cambio*) are available at banks and kiosks throughout the city, but especially around the station, Rialto and San Marco.
- American Express offers competitive exchange rates ➕ G12 ✉ Salizzada San Moisè, San Marco 1471 ☎ Emergency toll-free 1678/72 000 ☀ Summer: Mon–Sat 8–8. Rest of year: Mon–Fri 9–5:3; Sat 9–12:30

Places of worship

- Anglican: St George's ➕ E13 ✉ Campo San Vio, Dorsoduro 871 ☎ 041 520 0571
- Catholic (English mass): San Moisè ➕ G12 ✉ Campo San Moisè, San Marco; Basilica di San Marco ➕ G–H12 ✉ Piazza San Marco; I Gesuiti ➕ G–H10 ✉ Campo dei Gesuiti; Scalzi ➕ D10 ✉ Fondamenta degli Scalzi; Santi Giovanni e Paolo ➕ H11 ✉ Campo Santi Giovanni e Paolo; Redentore ➕ F15 ✉ Campo Redentore, Giudecca; San Giorgio Maggiore ➕ H14 ✉ Isola di San Giorgio Maggiore
- Jewish: ➕ E9 ✉ Ghetto Vecchio ☎ 041 715012

Women & student travellers

- Women visiting Venice on their own should have few problems in

the city, which is extremely safe, but parks and the station area should be avoided late at night.
- Discounts are available for student travellers in some city museums.

Time differences

- Italy is one hour ahead of British time, except for a brief period in October when they are the same (note that EU regulations may standardise hour changes).
- US Eastern Standard Time is six hours behind Italy, and Pacific Standard Time is nine hours behind.
- Sydney is eight hours ahead of Italy in summer.

Toilets

- Public conveniences are located at Piazzale Roma ➕ C11, the railway station ➕ C10–D10, the west side of Accademia bridge ➕ E13, off Campo San Bartolomeo ➕ G11, by the Giardinetti Reali ➕ G12–13, on Calle Erizzo near the church of San Martino ➕ J12, and in the Albergo Diurno (Day Hotel) on Ramo Primo a Ascensione ➕ G12.
- In bars and cafés ask for *il gabinetto* or *il bagno*.
- Do not confuse *signori* (men) with *signore* (women).

Electricity

- Current is 220v AC (50 cycles), but is suitable for 240-volt appliances.
- Plugs are of the Continental two-round-pin variety.

Etiquette

- Do not wear shorts, miniskirts or skimpy tops in churches.
- Do not intrude while church services are in progress.
- Do not eat or drink in churches.
- Many churches forbid the use of flashes, or may even ban photography altogether.
- There are few non-smoking areas

in restaurants or public places, but smoking is banned on public transport (including boats).

PUBLIC TRANSPORT

- Venice is a compact city, and the occasions when you need to use its public transport are surprisingly few. But while walking in such a beautiful place is an obvious pleasure, so, too, is the experience of taking a boat.

Public transport agency

- Venice's public transport is run by the Azienda del Consorzio Trasporti Veneziani (ACTV), with information offices in Piazzale Roma and Corte dell'Albero, San Marco 3880. Mainland buses and boats ☎ 041 528 7886

Boats

- ACTV runs two basic types of boat: the general-purpose *vaporetto*, and the faster *motoscafo*. Both follow set routes and are numbered – look for the number at the front of the boat. As the same number boat may run in two directions (up and down the Grand Canal, for example), it is vital at the quays – which usually have separate boarding points for each direction – to make sure you board a boat heading in the right direction. This is particularly true at the Ferrovia and San Zaccaria, both busy termini for several routes.
- The web of boat routes around Venice is not as confusing as it first seems. The basic route is Line 1 along the Grand Canal (Piazzale Roma–San Marco–Lido and back). Line 82 also follows the Grand Canal, but has fewer stops; lines 3 and 4 are faster summer-only services. A second 82 boat runs from San Zaccaria to Piazzale

Roma by way of the Giudecca. The other boat you may use is Line 12, which runs to the islands of Murano, Burano and Torcello from the Fondamente Nuove. The ferry information throughout this guide gives the nearest stop as well as the line number.

- Tickets can be bought at most landing stages, on board boats (with a surcharge), and at shops or tobacconists with an ACTV sticker. Tickets are valid only for the route for which they are issued; there is usually a flat fare along the length of the route so the price is the same for one stop or ten stops. Tickets, except those bought individually for Line 1, must be validated in machines at each landing stage before boarding. Heavy spot fines are levied if you are caught travelling without a ticket.
- Four tourist tickets are available: the *Biglietto 24 Ore*, valid on all lines for 24 hours; the *Biglietto 72 Ore*, valid for three days; the *Biglietto Isole*, valid for travel one way (with stopovers) on Line 12 to Murano, Burano and Torcello; and a 7-day ticket, also valid for the islands and ACTV buses to the airport.
- ACTV runs a reduced service throughout the night on most routes. Exact times are posted on timetables at every quay. Tickets can be bought on board.

Water taxis

- Venice's water taxis are fast but extremely expensive. The basic rate is around L35,000 for seven minutes, plus L500 for every additional 15 seconds. Surcharges are levied for each piece of luggage, for trips between 10PM and 7AM, and for each additional passenger over a maximum of four. You can hail a taxi on a canal, but it is usually easier to call by phone –

which means around L10,000 on the clock before you start ☎ 041 523 5775, 041 522 2303, 041 716124, 041 522 1265 or 041 523 0575; airport 041 541 5084

Taxis

• For journeys to and from the mainland there are taxi ranks at Piazzale Roma ☎ 041 523 7774; Marco Polo Airport ☎ 041 526 5975; and at the railway station at Mestre ☎ 041 929499. Otherwise, call Radio Taxi ☎ 041 936222

Traghetti

• As there are only three bridges across the Grand Canal, Venice's *traghetti* (ferries) provide an invaluable service. Using old gondolas, they ply back and forth at seven strategic points. Quays are usually obscure, so look out for the little yellow 'Traghetto' signs. Crossings currently cost L600, which you hand to the ferryman as you board. Venetians usually stand, but nobody minds if you sit unless the boat is crowded. Be careful with small children, and watch your balance when the boat pushes off.

MEDIA & COMMUNICATIONS

Telephones

• Telecom Italia (TI) provides public telephones in bars, on the streets and in TI offices. All are indicated by red or yellow signs showing a telephone dial and receiver. Venice has TI booths in Piazzale Roma ✚ C11 🕒 8AM–9:30PM and the main post office ✚ G11 ✉ Fondaco dei Tedeschi 🕒 8:15–7.

• Public phones accept L100, L200 and L500 coins, as well as the L200 *gettone* token. Most also accept phone cards (*schede telefoniche*), available in L5,000, L10,000 and L15,000 denominations from tobacconists, TI offices, automatic dispensers or shops displaying a TI sticker. Remember to tear the corner off the card before using it.

• Peak periods are weekdays 8–1, off-peak is 1–8, and calls are cheap at all other times. The cheap international rate covers the weekend and 8PM–8AM during the week.

• The dialling tone is alternating long and short pips. A series of rapid pips means you are being connected, while a series of long beeps indicates a ringing telephone at the other end. More rapid beeps means 'engaged'.

• For international calls, use a phone card or a *telefono a scatti* – a kiosk where you speak first and pay when your call is over (found in some bars, hotels, post offices and tourist offices, and in most TI offices). Dial 00 for an international line followed by the country code. The code for Italy when calling from abroad is 39.

• To make a reverse-charge (collect) call, dial 15 (Europe) or 170 (intercontinental) and ask to make *una chiamata con pagamento a destinazione*.

• The area code for Venice is 041, and must be used when calling from outside or within Venice (numbers in this book include the code).

Post offices

• Venice's central post office (*posta* or *ufficio postale*) is near the Rialto bridge ✚ G11 ✉ Palazzo delle Poste, Fondaco dei Tedeschi ☎ 041 522 0606 🕒 Mon–Sat 8–7; foreign exchange (upstairs) 8–6.

• Another larger office lies just west of Piazza San Marco ✚ G12 ✉ Calle dell'Ascensione ☎ 041 528 5949 🕒 Mon–Fri 8:10–1:30; Sat 8:10–12:30.

• Stamps (*francobolli*) are available from post offices, or from tobacconists (*tabacchi*) displaying a blue 'T' sign.

- Post-boxes are small and red and are marked *Poste* or *Lettere*. They usually have two slots – one for local mail (*Città*), the other for destinations further afield (*Altre Destinazione*).
- International mail sent to and from Venice can take up to three weeks to arrive. You can speed things up by sending post *espresso* (express) or *raccomandata* (registered).
- Address poste restante letters Fermo Posta, Fondaco dei Tedeschi, 30100 Venezia. Mail can be collected Mon–Sat 8:15AM–7PM. Take a passport when collecting mail and be prepared to pay a small fee. Filing can be haphazard, so ask staff to check under both your first and last names.

Telex & telegrams
- These can be sent from Venice's main post office or by calling 186, or 170 for international telegrams.

Newspapers & magazines
- Venice's two main local newspapers are *Il Gazzettino* and *La Nuova Venezia*. Both contain listings for the city.
- Quality national papers include the centre-left *La Repubblica* and centre-right *Corriere della Sera*.
- *Corriere dello Sport* and the *Gazzetta dello Sport*, two exclusively sports-based papers, are also popular.
- News magazines (*riviste*) such as *L'Espresso* and *Panorama* also enjoy a large readership.
- Foreign newspapers are readily available in Venice, usually from late afternoon on the day of issue. Kiosks at the railway station are the best source.

Radio & television
- Italian radio and television offer many deregulated national and local stations, including several based in the Veneto region around Venice. Major national television stations divide between the channels of the state RAI network (RAI 1, 2 and 3) and the channels founded by Silvio Berlusconi (Canale 5, Rete 4 and Italia Uno).

EMERGENCIES

Crime
- Venice's many tourists are an obvious target for the unscrupulous, but by using common sense and taking a few precautions you should stay safe. Report thefts to your hotel and then to the main police station, which has a department to deal with visitors' problems ⊠ Questura, Via San Nicolodi 22, Marghera ☎ 041 271 5511. They will issue you with a document (*una denuncia*) to send in with your insurance claims. Report lost passports to the police and your consulate or embassy.
- For police in an emergency, telephone 112 or 113.
- Carry cash in a belt or pouch, never in a pocket.
- Do not carry large amounts of cash. Use credit cards or travellers' cheques.
- Wear your camera and never put it down on café tables. Beware of strap-cutting thieves.
- Do not flaunt valuables. Better still, leave them at home.
- Leave jewellery in the hotel safe (not in rooms), especially items such as chains and earrings which can easily be snatched.
- Hold bags across your front, not just hung over one shoulder where they can be grabbed.
- Beware of pickpockets wherever groups of tourists gather.
- After dark, avoid non-commercial parts of the city, parks and the area around the railway station.

- Always lock your car, and never leave luggage, cameras or valuables inside.

Consulates

- Australia ✉ Via Alessandria 215, Rome ☎ 06/852 721
- Austria ✉ Santa Croce 251 ☎ 041 524 0556
- Belgium ✉ San Marco 1470 ☎ 041 522 4124
- Canada ✉ Via G B Rossi 27, Rome ☎ 06/445 981
- Denmark ✉ San Marco 466/g ☎ 041 520 0822
- France ✉ Záttere 1397 ☎ 041 522 4319
- Netherlands ✉ San Marco 423 ☎ 041 528 3416
- Norway ✉ Santa Croce 466/b ☎ 041 523 1345
- Republic of Ireland ✉ Piazza Campitelli 3, Rome ☎ 06/697 9121
- Switzerland ✉ Zattere, Dorsoduro 810 ☎ 041 520 3944 or 041 522 5996
- UK ✉ Via San Paolo 7, Milan ☎ 02/723 001
- USA ✉ Via Principe Amedeo 2/10, Milan ☎ 02/290 351

Emergency phone numbers

- Emergency services (police, fire and ambulance) ☎ 113
- Police (*Carabinieri*) ☎ 112
- Questura (Venice Police Station) ☎ 041 271 5511
- Fire (*Vigili di Fuoco*) ☎ 115/113
- Ambulance ☎ 041 523 0000
- Hospital and first aid (Ospedale Civile) ☎ 041 529 4517

Lost property

- City streets ☎ 041 270 8225 or 041 520 8844
- Buses or boats ☎ 041 272 2111/2179
- Train or station ☎ 041 785238
- Airport ☎ 041 260 6436
- Report losses of passports to the police and your consulate.
- Report general losses to the main police station ✉ Questura, Via San Nicolodi 22, Marghera ☎ 041 271 5511

Health

- Likely hazards include too much sun, air pollution and biting insects.
- Water is safe to drink unless marked *acqua non potabile*.
- Condoms (*profilatici*) are available over the counter from chemists and most supermarkets.
- Take out health insurance before travelling and keep any receipts for medicine and treatment. Free treatment is available to citizens of EU countries, but to be eligible you must take form E111.
- Pharmacies (*una farmacia*) are identified by a green cross and have the same opening hours as shops, but open late on some days as displayed on pharmacy doors. Staff can give advice on minor ailments and dispense many medicines over the counter, including some only available on prescription in other countries. Remember to bring any prescriptions that might be required to obtain medicine.
- If you wish to see a doctor (*un medico*), enquire at your hotel or call ☎ 041 531 4481. For first aid (*pronto soccorso*) or hospital treatment, visit the Ospedale Civile ✚ H10–H11 ✉ Campo Santi Giovanni e Paolo ☎ 041 529 4517
- Vaccinations are unnecessary for entry into Italy unless you are travelling from a known infected area. Check current requirements if you are travelling from the Far East, Africa, South America or the Middle East.

LANGUAGE

- Italians respond well to foreigners who make an effort to speak their language, however badly. Many Italians speak at least some English, and most upmarket hotels and restaurants have multi-lingual staff.

- All Italian words are pronounced as written, with each vowel and consonant sounded. The letter *c* is hard, as in English 'cat', except when followed by *i* or *e*, when it becomes the soft ch of 'children'. The same applies to *g* when followed by *i* or *e* – soft in *giardino*, as in the English 'giant'; hard in *gatto*, as in 'gate'. Words ending in *o* are almost always masculine in gender (plural ending – *i*); those ending in *a* are feminine (plural ending – *e*).
- Use the polite, third person (*lei*) to speak to strangers and the second person (*tu*) to friends or children.

Courtesies

good morning buon giorno
good afternoon/good evening buona sera
good night buona notte
hello/goodbye (informal) ciao
hello (answering the telephone) pronto
goodbye arrivederci
please per favore
thank you (very much) (mille) grazie
you're welcome prego
how are you? (polite/informal) come sta/stai?
I'm fine sto bene
I'm sorry mi dispiace
excuse me/I beg your pardon mi scusi
excuse me (in a crowd) permesso

Basic vocabulary

yes sì
no no
I do not understand no ho capito
left/right sinistra/destra
entrance entrata
exit uscita
open/closed aperto/chiuso
upstairs sopra
downstairs da basso

inside dentro
come in! avanti!
good/bad buono/cattivo
big/small grande/piccolo
with con
without senza
less/more meno/più
near vicino
far lontano
hot/cold caldo/freddo
early presto
late ritardo
here qui
there là
now adesso
later più tardi
today oggi
tomorrow domani
yesterday ieri
morning mattino
afternoon pomeriggio
how much is it? quant'è?
expensive caro
cheap a buon mercato
when? quando?
do you have …? avete …?

Emergencies

help! aiuto!
where is the nearest telephone? dov'è il telefono più vicino?
there has been an accident c'è stato un incidente
call the police chiamate la polizia
call a doctor/an ambulance chiamate un medico/un'ambulanza
first aid pronto soccorso
where is the nearest hospital? dov'è l'ospedale più vicino?

Numbers

one uno, una
two due
three tre
four quattro
five cinque
six sei
seven sette
eight otto
nine nove

93

INDEX

CityPack
Venice

Written by   Tim Jepson
Edited, designed and produced by AA Publishing

Maps   © The Automobile Association 1997, 1999
Fold-out map © RV Reise- und Verkehrsverlag Munich · Stuttgart
© Cartography: GeoData

Distributed in the United Kingdom by AA Publishing, Norfolk House, Priestley Road, Basingstoke, Hampshire, RG24 9NY.

The contents of this publication are believed correct at the time of printing. Nevertheless, the publishers cannot be held responsible for any errors or omissions or for changes in the details given in this guide or for the consequences of any reliance on the information provided by the same. Assessments of attractions, hotels, restaurants and so forth are based upon the author's own personal experience and, therefore, descriptions given in this guide necessarily contain an element of subjective opinion which may not reflect the publishers' opinion or dictate a reader's own experiences on another occasion.

We have tried to ensure accuracy in this guide, but things do change and we would be grateful if readers would advise us of any inaccuracies they may encounter.

A CIP catalogue record for this book is available from the British Library.

ISBN 0 7495 2224 0

Published by AA Publishing (a trading name of Automobile Association Developments Limited, whose registered office is Norfolk House, Priestley Road, Basingstoke, Hampshire RG24 9NY. Registered number 1878835).

Colour separation by Daylight Colour Art Pte Ltd, Singapore
Printed and bound by Dai Nippon Printing Co (Hong Kong) Ltd.

Acknowledgements
The Automobile Association wishes to thank the following photographers and libraries for their assistance in the preparation of this book:
The Bridgeman Art Library Ltd, London 31a Supper at the House of Levi, 1573 by Veronese, (Paolo Caliari), Galleria dell'Accademia, Venice, 50 The Miracle of the Cross on San Lorenzo Bridge, 1500 by Gentile Bellini, Galleria dell'Accademia, Venice, 51b St George Killing the Dragon by Carpaccio, Vittore, Scuola di San Giorgio degli Schiavoni, Venice; Mary Evans Picture Library 12a, 12b, 12c; John Hesteltine Archive 42; Spectrum Colour Library 24b.
The remaining photographs are held in the Association's own photo library (AA PHOTO LIBRARY) and were taken by Dario Mitidieri, pages 5a, 8, 16, 18, 20a, 20b, 21, 27b, 28, 29a, 30a, 30b, 33a, 35a, 37a, 37b, 39a, 43a, 43b, 45, 46, 49b, 51a, 53, 54, 55b, 57, 58, 59; Richard Newton, pages 23a, 32b, 52a; Clive Sawyer, pages 1, 5b, 6/7, 13a, 13b, 15, 17, 19, 23b, 24a, 25, 26, 27a, 29b, 33b, 34a, 34b, 35b, 36, 38a, 38b, 39b, 40a, 40b, 41a, 41b, 44a, 44b, 47b, 48a, 48b, 49a, 52b, 55a, 56, 60, 63a, 63b, 87a, 87b and Rosie Walford, pages 32a and 47a.

Cover photographs
Main picture: Zefa Pictures Ltd. Inset top: AA Photo Library (Clive Sawyer)
Inset bottom: AA Photo Library (Dario Mitidieri)

SECOND EDITION UPDATED BY *Tim Jepson*

Titles in the CityPack series
● Amsterdam ● Atlanta ● Bangkok ● Barcelona ● Beijing ● Berlin ● Boston ●
● Brussels & Bruges ● Chicago ● Dublin ● Florence ● Hong Kong ● Istanbul ●
● Lisbon ● London ● Los Angeles ● Madrid ● Miami ● Montréal ● Moscow ●
● Munich ● New York ● Paris ● Prague ● Rome ● San Francisco ● Seattle ●
● Shanghai ● Singapore ● Sydney ● Tokyo ● Toronto ● Venice ● Vienna ●
● Washington ●